Let Go

Seven Stumbling Blocks to Christian Discipleship

Casey Cole, OFM

franciscan
media
Cincinnati, Ohio

Scripture texts in this work are taken from the New American Bible, revised edition © 2010, 1991, 1986, 1970 Confraternity of Christian Doctrine, Washington, D.C. and are used by permission of the copyright owner. All Rights Reserved. No part of the New American Bible may be reproduced in any form without permission in writing from the copyright owner.

Cover design by LUCAS Art & Design—Jenison, MI
Book design by Mark Sullivan

ISBN 978-1-63253-300-5
Copyright ©2020, by Casey Cole, OFM. All rights reserved.
Published by Franciscan Media
28 W. Liberty St.
Cincinnati, OH 45202
www.FranciscanMedia.org

Printed in the United States of America
Printed on acid-free paper
20 21 22 23 24 5 4 3 2

contents

What Must I do?

As he was setting out on a journey, a man ran up, knelt down before him, and asked him, "Good teacher, what must I do to inherit eternal life?" Jesus answered him, "Why do you call me good? No one is good but God alone. You know the commandments: 'You shall not kill; you shall not commit adultery; you shall not steal; you shall not bear false witness; you shall not defraud; honor your father and your mother.'" He replied and said to him, "Teacher, all of these I have observed from my youth." Jesus, looking at him, loved him and said to him, "You are lacking in one thing. Go, sell what you have, and give to the poor and you will have treasure in heaven; then come, follow me." At that statement his face fell, and he went away sad, for he had many possessions.

—MARK 10: 17-22

The story of the rich young man is among the most popular in the Bible. Found in all three of the synoptic Gospels, Christians are reminded with regularity of the young man's attachment to possessions—and preached at about their own possessions. The problem, we often hear, is that wealth corrupts and so attachment to money prevents us from inheriting eternal life. This man was so concerned with how much money he had, so unwilling to give it up, that he passed up on eternal life to keep it. We should learn from his mistake, we are told, donating more to charity and living a simple life.

That's great advice. But it misses the larger point. As much as this passage is about turning from inordinate attachments to wealth in order to live more simply, it has a far more essential theme: discipleship. Jesus doesn't tell the man he must sell all he has because this is a nonnegotiable requirement to enter heaven. We know from the Gospels Jesus doesn't demand this of everyone he encounters: Zacchaeus sells only *half* of his possessions and is praised for it; the women that follow after the disciples tending their needs are never asked to sell anything; Jesus even defends the woman who uses the expensive perfumed oil to anoint him when she is criticized for *not* selling her possessions and giving to the poor. No, the reason that Jesus tells the man *he* must sell all that he has is precisely because this is what prevented *him* from being a true disciple and depending entirely on Jesus. The man was bound to his possessions, clung to them too tightly, and so would never be able to follow Jesus with his whole heart. The fact that the man goes away sad, giving up a chance to follow Jesus, proves Jesus's insistence that he must let them go: His possessions got in the way of his quest for eternal life.

But that may not be the case for you. It's certainly not the case for me.

While we could all probably be a little less dependent on money and possessions, the fact of the matter is many of us have far greater stumbling blocks to discipleship than money; many of us carry far heavier burdens than our possessions. The purpose of this book is to place you at the feet of Jesus to ask the same question as the rich young man: "Lord, what must I do to inherit eternal life? What is getting in my way of following you unreservedly, of handing myself completely over to your will and being your disciple?" I can hardly think of a more important question in any of our lives.

No doubt, sin in all of its forms plays a major role in this, and multiple volumes can and have been written through the lens of moral theology. That is not my lens here. What I want to focus on in these pages are the ordinary events of our lives, the day-to-day inter-actions that often do not get the attention they deserve. I'm talking about things that are not inherently sinful, things that might even be *good* in another person but create a distortion in our lives. Some of us may need to let go of money to follow Jesus, but for others, grandiose views of self, unfair expectations, and trivial worries do far more damage to a life of discipleship than anything else. Some of us need to let go of possessions, but others have too strong a grip on safety nets, past traumas, or petty grudges to be free enough to follow Jesus. Truly, nothing is too small or too insignificant. *Anything* that prevents us from following Jesus with our whole heart, anything that holds us back, is a stumbling block to Christian discipleship as deadly as sin. If we refuse to let go of whatever it is, we run the risk of ending up just like the rich young man: sad and far from Jesus.

Naturally, no single book could possibly contain every stumbling block that could ever get in our way, and this one does not plan to try. What I provide here is not an exhaustive checklist of faults, nor a complete examination of conscience, but a primer for the pump. What I want from this book is for people to look at their lives and ask themselves, "What would Jesus tell me to let go of in order to follow him?" In looking at my life and reflecting on what I have struggled with thus far, I have come up with seven categories of stumbling blocks I believe get in the way for most people because we choose to cling to them rather than live freely. Within each cate-gory are three forms that each stumbling block can take, examples of how I have experienced them in my life, all with with the same exhortation: Let go.

- Let go of all that does not bring life.
- Let go of all that holds you back.
- Let go of all that gets in the way of Christian discipleship.

An infinite number of things will bring us comfort, satisfaction, and even happiness, and they may be good for a while. But only one thing can bring us eternal joy: following Jesus Christ and becoming a part of his mission. Jesus wants each and every one of us to be his disciples. He wants us to let go of anything and everything that gets in the way of following him, that prevents us from trusting completely, that holds us back from throwing ourselves headlong into the mission. As Pope Francis reminds us in his apostolic exhortation *Gaudete et Exsultate*, "The Lord asks everything of us, and in return he offers us true life, the happiness for which we were created. He wants us to be saints and not to settle for a bland and mediocre existence" (#1). Being a disciple of Christ is not a part-time job. It is not something we do distracted, with half our effort, simply to get it done. It's not simply about joining a church or accepting Jesus as our "Lord and Savior," nor is it enough to profess with our lips what we believe. Being his disciple means transforming every aspect of our lives so that nothing, not even the smallest part of who we are, is out of touch with the mission of Christ. It's about giving *every ounce of our being* to the God who created us, taking up whatever we are called to do, whenever we are called to do it, without hesitation. We cannot do that if we are busy holding onto something else, saving something to the side "in case this doesn't work out." God wants *everything* from us, and so we're either fully in, or we're not in at all.

Let go of what holds you back, and live completely in the freedom of being a disciple of Christ.

chapter one

Self

Then Jesus said to his disciples, "Whoever wishes to come after me must deny himself, take up his cross, and follow me. For whoever wishes to save his life will lose it, but whoever loses his life for my sake will find it. What profit would there be for one to gain the whole world and forfeit his life? Or what can one give in exchange for his life?

—MATTHEW 16: 24-28

I have moved many times in my life. Twelve times, in fact. Twelve times in the past sixteen years I have packed up everything I owned, driven to another city, and essentially started life over. While many would see this as a tremendous hassle, a constant inconvenience of living in transition, I have always found it to be a rather exciting opportunity. As difficult as saying goodbye to people and places that we love can be, moving also affords us the chance to say goodbye to the people and places that have caused us distress. Entering a new city with a new job and forming new friends is the closest we will ever come to a blank slate in life, an opportunity to start fresh and to live how we've always wanted. With every move, I can't help but be optimistic for the future. Things are going to be different this time, and for the better. *What an absolutely hopeful experience.*

And sometimes they are. Sometimes I am at a place in my life where a change in scenery does me good, when hitting the "reset" button on my routine is exactly what I needed to better live as a disciple of Christ.

But sometimes, unfortunately, they're not. Sometimes, no matter how hopeful I am about the future and the many changes I want to make in my life, within a few months I find myself back exactly where I was before. Despite changing my address, my job, and the people around me, despite my efforts to run away from the problems that brought me down and got in the way of serving the Lord, the problems I faced before tend to be the same problems I face in the new place. It is as if they followed me; as if they jumped into one of my boxes and I unknowingly took them with me.

For years this frustrated me. Hope inevitably turned to disappointment. I couldn't understand why, no matter how many times I moved, the same problems kept happening. Then a spiritual director shared an old quip: "Wherever you go, there you are." As much as we would like to place the blame for our problems on some external factor—pointing our finger in accusation against another and convincing ourselves that if it were not for that factor, if only we could escape that one thing, our lives would be better—the cause of our problems often lies within us. It doesn't matter where we live, what we do for a living, or who we associate with, we cannot run from ourselves. If we have anger in our hearts, we can run from our past enemies, but we will most certainly find new people with whom to fight. If we struggle with authority, we can change jobs, but we will undoubtedly have new problems at our next one. As the great modern contemplative Thomas Merton once wrote, "If you go out into the desert merely to get away from people you dislike, you will find neither peace nor solitude; you will only isolate yourself with a tribe of devils" (*New Seeds of Contemplation,* 52). When the problem is with our very self, we will bring it wherever we go.

If we want to be disciples of Jesus Christ, following him in complete freedom and without any reservation, the first and most important thing that we must let go of is ourselves. We must identify all that lives within us that does not bear life, that does not reflect the joy of the kingdom, that does not live up to the person Christ created us to be, and we must die to ourselves. Let go of your delusions of grandeur, self-loathing, and false selves, and follow Christ as the person he created you to be.

Delusions of Grandeur

Eighty percent of people believe themselves to be above-average drivers. That's a fact. It's also true that 90 percent of professors believe themselves to be above-average teachers and 85 percent of students believe that they are better than average at getting along with others. Being that only 50 percent of people can technically be above the "average," what each of these statistics shows is that people have a tendency to overestimate their own abilities, believing themselves to be far more competent at something than they actually are. Compounding the problem and adding a bit of irony is the fact that one needs some level of expertise to be competent enough to evaluate one's skills, and so those who have the least ability are often the ones with the most inflated sense of self. In so many cases, we don't know enough to know that we don't know!

On one level, this is nothing more than a benign human experience we can easily forgive: Is there really that much wrong with having a *slightly* inflated sense of self? So, we tell people we're a few inches taller than we actually are. We have a bit more confidence than we should. Given the challenges of our world, one could even argue that a little extra confidence, a slightly inflated belief in oneself, even if not founded in reality, might be the very thing we need to act in the face of difficulty. A bit of a lie, for sure, but maybe a lie that helps us do what we otherwise wouldn't have even tried.

If only it were just *a bit* of a lie. More often, what happens is the lie we tell about ourselves, that inflated sense of who we are and what we're capable of, reaches the point of delusion. When we tell the same lie about ourselves often enough, we begin to believe it, and the vision we have of ourselves gets completely disconnected from the reality of who God has created us to be.

What's interesting about these situations, at least in my life, is that they often begin not from an inflated ego, but from self-doubt. When I think of the times and ways that I have come off as arrogant, believing myself to be better at something than I actually am, talking down to others, or outright thinking I am without flaws, I find that often behind my delusion is some serious self-consciousness. Rather than accept the person that I am—flawed and occasionally awkward—it is much more preferable to project a better version of myself. What is it we say all the time in situations of doubt? "Fake it 'til you make it." If we project a sense of confidence in what we do, even if we're completely lost and doubting our every move, we will eventually rise to the person we present ourselves to be—or at least trick others into believing that is who we really are.

Welcome to my teenage years. Welcome to just about every social situation of my life. I can't say exactly when it was, but at some point in my life, I simply decided to exude confidence regardless of how I felt. Rather than show discomfort or let people know that I was in any way less than perfect, I began to project an air of coolness I thought people would like. I pretended that everything was under control when it was not; I avoided anything I was not good at, hiding my flaws in order to present myself as someone who could excel at everything. I refused help even when I needed it; I spoke first and most boldly, sticking by my first answer, assuring others that I knew what I was talking about. And it worked. Friends told me that I had a nonchalance that was so cool. People trusted what I had to say, and even came to me for help. People expected me to be competent and reliable at whatever I did. I looked the part, and so I got the part.

There was just one problem: I was pretending. Well, at least I was at first. What started as as a projection of my ideal self eventually became who I thought I truly was; what started as a defense mechanism against my doubts occasionally revealed itself as arrogance and overconfidence. *I'm unflappable. I'm good at everything. I don't need help. I can do it all on my own.* While I would have never actually said these words aloud, and even though my actions only reflected these sentiments from time to time, something inside me began to believe they were true. Hiding my flaws from others made me believe, even if ever so slightly, that I was nearly without flaws. The lie had crept into my sense of self.

More than a slight miscalculation of self-awareness, there were parts of me—and no doubt, there are parts of us all—that had grown into a delusion of grandeur. Left unchecked and grown out of control, these can be damaging to ourselves, and more importantly, the mission of Christ. It is one thing to hide our flaws from others, not wanting to be completely vulnerable with everyone we meet. It is another thing to believe that we are without flaws. The fact of the matter is that we are weak. We are vulnerable. We need tremendous help just to survive the day. Everything we have and everything we do is the result of Jesus loving us first, of him giving us the strength we need to continue. When we hide our flaws even from ourselves, believing even for a second that we don't have any or that our flaws are so minuscule that we do not need help from anyone, that we possess within ourselves all the strength we will ever need to live a happy and healthy life, we unwittingly cut ourselves off from the true source of strength: the grace of the Holy Spirit. If we don't think we need help, we'll never feel compelled to ask for it. What a shame it would be to stop asking God for help.

It is one thing to exude confidence in our answers when faced with difficult questions, letting people believe we are more knowledgeable than we actually are. It is another thing to believe we know everything. The fact of the matter is we know very little about the world. We aren't perfect. We make tons of mistakes on a regular basis. When we forget these things, allowing ourselves to believe that we actually are experts on life, we run the risk of losing our humility, of being unable to accept new information, and, worst of all, becoming a judge of everyone we meet. Those who do not check their delusions of grandeur inevitably place themselves above others, lording their perceived gifts over the very people they should be serving.

It is one thing to believe we can help others even when we are in over our heads. It is another thing to believe we are the savior everyone has been waiting for. The fact of the matter is we are human, just like everyone else. We did not die for anyone's sins. We are just as much in need of saving as the ones we serve. Too often, especially when we have been blessed with a caring heart and are applauded for our pastoral skills, we can delude ourselves into thinking that what the world needs is us, that if the world had *my* leadership, *my* preaching, *my* words of wisdom, everything would be better. This is an enormous lie. The world does not need us to be its savior, especially not when all we can offer is ourselves. What the world needs is Jesus Christ, the incarnate God, the one who gave his life for the life of the world. The one who came to be like us so that we can become like him. The world already has a savior, and we do everyone a disservice, including ourselves, when we try to take his place.

Ultimately, is that not precisely what our delusions of grandeur are? When we see ourselves as far more skilled and important than we actually are, we cease to act as the person God created us to be and instead begin to take on the very role of God. We believe ourselves to be flawless, so act as the judge of all. We believe ourselves to be strong, so we act as the savior of everyone we meet. Without even realizing it, we forget our place in the world and try to take over God's.

We cannot follow Christ when we already see ourselves in his place. If we want to be his disciple, we must let go of our inflated sense of self, our savior complex, our arrogance, our belief that we do not need help from anyone, and our implicit desire to be everyone's judge. We must take up the humility to place ourselves beneath Jesus, accept our faults and flaws, and begin to act like the people we were created to be: servants of God.

Denial of Goodness

Just as it is dangerous to have an inflated sense of self, replacing God with ourselves, the opposite is also something to avoid: denying the very goodness God has created in us. How often do we view our nature as something inferior, flawed, and altogether worthless? Focusing only on the sins we commit, we fail to recognize the unfathomable good of which we are capable. How often do we make a mistake and blame it on the fact that we are "only human"? For the life of me, I have never been able to understand why we say this as if it were a bad thing. Humans are the only creatures created in the image and likeness of God. We are capable of complex speech and abstract thoughts. We wield tremendous power over our environment, producing extraordinary technological advances. Of all of the creatures on earth, we are the only ones that seem to know that we are created and loved by God and return that love through imitation, worship, and self-sacrifice. "Only human"? We insult God by denying the beauty of his creation.

In a very practical sense, we do this when we refuse to accept compliments. Someone notices something we've done, makes the effort to point out how pleasing that thing is to them, and what do we do? We try to diminish it. We dissociate ourselves from it. We might even deny our responsibility at all. *Oh, no, it's no big deal. I really didn't do anything.* When you think about it, it is probably the rudest thing we could do in the situation and it certainly does not reflect an appropriate sense of ourselves as God created us.

So why do we do it?

It may come from a false sense of humility within us. Knowing that it is not very "Christian" to be arrogant or proud of one's accomplishments, we immediately become embarrassed in the face of a compliment and seek to distance ourselves from it. We believe that in denying the compliment we are acting humbly, lowering ourselves before others, but the truth is ironically the opposite: We reveal our arrogance in believing that the compliment was ours to deny. You see, in becoming embarrassed and thinking that we need to distance ourselves from the affirmation, we reveal that we have too closely associated the goodness of the situation with our own doing. In hearing a compliment about who we are or what we have done, we forget we did not achieve this good thing, but that all goodness comes from God. Denying a compliment can be an arrogant act of false humility, denying what God has done in us. Those who are truly humble can receive compliments without any discomfort or need to deny because they have no attachment to the words: They recognize all glory is rightfully God's.

Of course, this is not always the case. Some people refuse compliments because they have a negative view of self. This is also a case of too closely associating the compliment with our own actions, but the problem is compounded with some degree of self-loathing. We believe ourselves to be unworthy of such compliments, and so we dismiss the other's words as untrue. *No, I'm not good at anything. I don't deserve compliments.* We cannot believe such things about ourselves, and so our only response is to deny them.

Some people are simply uncomfortable with who they are. This might be the result of a condition they have experienced from birth, a physical or psychological characteristic that distinguishes them from others and leaves them feeling self-conscious. *I'm different from everyone else.* I meet people all the time who struggle with an issue of body image or sexuality, feeling something about them is intrinsically wrong. *I hate the way I look. I'm disgusting to everyone.* Others don't think they have the right abilities or talents and they let what they can't do define their entire self-worth. *I'm so stupid, I'll never be good at anything.* These feelings might be rooted in childhood environments, experiences with parents or peers, or social expectations. Sometimes it's simply a personality issue.

It is difficult to see the glory of God in yourself when you don't think you are capable of goodness. And what a burden this is for someone seeking to be a disciple of Christ. People who do not believe they can be loved by others and are not able to see the goodness of God in themselves can begin to believe that they are not *worthy* of love, that they are *unforgivable*, that they are, in fact, *worthless* in the eyes of God. They refuse the very call to discipleship. One can imagine them saying, "What could Christ do with me anyway? There is nothing I can offer the kingdom. I would just mess everything up." When we refuse to accept that God can work wonders through us, it is going to be next to impossible to be his disciple.

If we want to follow Jesus where he's leading us, we need to let go of our false humility, self-loathing, self-doubt, and refusal to accept what is good in our lives. These are lies, burdens that will only weigh us down. We cannot take them with us. This is easy to say, much more difficult to do. Don't be afraid to seek help if you're aware of any of these issues in your own life. A good place to begin is to seriously consider this message: If we want to follow Jesus, we must accept that God has created us good, that we are loved beyond all imagining, and that, even though we may have some faults, God is capable of extraordinary things in us. Let Jesus lead, and give him all the glory.

False Selves

Just as a building may have a front façade, a false wall that gives the impression it is something that it is not, so too can we have "false selves" that hide who we really are. This can be through flattery, as in the case of our delusions of grandeur, or in self-loathing, as in our denial of goodness, but they need not be so extreme, nor do they have to be entirely made-up. Anything that we claim as our identity or use to measure our worth—good, bad, or neutral—that is not essential to who God created us to be can become a false self for us.

The best example of this today might be our social media personas. As much as we like to think they are extensions of ourselves, and as truthful as we feel we are being, what we share never truly captures who we are. Even if we are not photoshopping our pictures so we look younger and thinner, intentionally trying to deceive people, and even if our posts are about things that really happened, our profiles are highly curated version of our lives: we choose what to share, and more importantly, what to withhold. The world only sees pictures taken at the perfect angle; our cyber friends only see videos if we look and sound exactly how we want to be perceived. Our online personas are real in that they depict a part of who we are, but they are also superficial (if not completely fake) in that they present a self—well put together, always in a good mood, never struggling, free of worries—that does not exist. This is not without consequence.

As someone who spends more time online than the average person, trust me when I say that not only will people begin to expect you to be someone you are not, you will find a growing conflict between your real self who can wear sweatpants and be normal, and your internet self that becomes someone else for the camera.

For those not on social media, this might sound like the most shallow thing you have ever heard. *Kids these days, right?* So it would seem, until we realize that this is just an extension of the way each and every one of us acts in our normal lives. Like it or not, we act differently depending on where we are or who we're around. Over the years, we have learned what is expected of us in certain situations, what will bring us the most success, what will help us most fit in, and so we adapt who we are when needed.

Our intention is not to deceive. There is nothing malicious about it! Many of us do so genuinely and unintentionally, naturally gravitating toward those around us out of a sense of hospitality and a desire for connection. And yet, the result is the same: In our desire to please others, we unwittingly project a version of ourselves that is not entirely authentic, going through life as a *series* of selves navigating the world. This can be exhausting, but it can also be fairly confusing. Those who spend their whole lives trying to please others, becoming who they need to be in each new situation, may struggle at times to remember who the "real" person inside them really is. Like someone who has dyed their hair so many times that they've forgotten what they naturally look like, so too can we forget who our true self is.

This was the case for someone I knew many years ago. He struggled with issues of mental illness, and believed he had to present himself to others as energetic, optimistic, and overly masculine, qualities that he most certainly did not have. He put on a happy face no matter the situation and tried to hide the person he really was inside.

For years, he seemed to function relatively fine. He may have even been comfortable with the person he was pretending to be. But it was a lie, and you can't live a lie forever. In the end he broke down and ended up doing tremendous damage to himself.

Sometimes the false self that we hide behind is not so much a fake persona we've created, but rather an inordinate or distorted relationship with a real part of ourselves. When we become fixated on an inconsequential part of who we are and make it our defining feature above all else, we also create a false self. Essentially we are idolizing a single aspect of ourselves.

To see what I mean, take my full name as I sign it on official documents: "Fr. Casey Cole, OFM." That is a lot of identities! Besides my first name, there is a title, "Father," that describes what I do and my place in the Church; a surname, "Cole," that assigns me a familial identity and history that can hardly be separated from class, status, and national origin; and a religious affiliation, marked by "OFM," indicating my social standing and lifestyle. Each of these designations says something very real and very important *about* me, but that does not mean that they necessarily *define* me. They are qualifiers, descriptors, additions to who I am and what I do, but they can never replace the central identity of "Casey." When we try to do so, conflating our titles, familial relations, or social statuses with who we essentially are, what results is a false self: Our sense of identity is based in transitory qualities. They can change, and when they do, we'll be left questioning who we really are.

For so many, this happens when we too closely define who we are by what we do. We look at our careers, activities, hobbies—whatever it is that we spend the most time doing—and we make it our central identity. In doing so, we no longer see ourselves as unique and complex individuals who happen to *do* something; we are what we do. *I'm a cardiovascular surgeon. I'm an athlete. I'm a helper.* This can have a damaging effect on our sense of self. Because we value productivity and usefulness so much in our society, seeing ourselves as nothing more than what we do places all of our self-worth in what we do and how well we do it. This might be great when we're successful, but it will ultimately fail. The hardest workers run out of energy and must ask for help themselves; even the most talented lose their edge and are pushed aside by newcomers. What then?

For seventeen of my first twenty-two years of life, I played baseball. It was the most important part of my life, the thing I was most proud of, and the way I defined who I was. *I am a baseball player.* And then I graduated college. All of a sudden, there were no more games to play, nothing to train for. A tear in my shoulder began to cause immense pain and signal the final blow to what was already a devastating reality: My life of playing baseball was over. For seventeen years, that had been who I was, the way I defined myself. Now it was gone, and there was a part of me that had to wonder: Who am I now? The false self I had propped up, the one I had used to define who I was in this world, had fallen. Baseball had been an important part of my life, but like anything we *do*, it did not define who I truly was.

The most transitory characteristic of our lives, and by far the most shallow form of our false selves, is the self defined by what others say of us. How often as children did we let our popularity shape the way we saw ourselves? How often, *even as adults*, do we let the many voices of society dictate what we're worth? Whether it be notions of beauty, intelligence, importance, usefulness, or success, there will always be people out there trying to tell us who we are and what we need to do to be loved. Resist them. Any voice that tries to convince us that our true self is incomplete or inadequate without the newest fad, that tries to make us into something that we are not, is not the voice of truth. To live our lives based on what others think of us or want us to do is the epitome of a false self. It is a mask that we might wear, but it does nothing but hide who we truly are.

Jesus does not want masks. He does not want projections of our superficial selves that bear no resemblance to who we really are. When he calls us to follow after him, he does not want the person we wish we were or the person we pretend to be. No, when he calls us, he wants the person he created, the person we are becoming in his love, our truest selves. If we want to follow after him, we must strip ourselves of everything that is superficial, inauthentic, forced, or pretend. We need to let go of all those partial and superficial selves. They just get in the way.

Truly Ourselves

Have you ever stopped to marvel at how amazingly unique you are? I don't mean in an inflated sense, as in our delusions of grandeur, but in the mere odds of it all. At the time of writing this, there are than 7.5 billion people in the world, and none of them is quite like you. From the color of your eyes to the shape your nose, from the way you walk to what you dream about, you are a complex combination of features that exists nowhere else in time and space than where you are. No one ever has been or ever will be the you that you are. That is remarkable.

More importantly, have you ever stopped to wonder *why*? Is God just really bad at creating humans, unable to create the perfect specimen but resigned to keep trying? Hardly. We know, of course, that God does not make mistakes, that even what we might perceive as defective or evil is still the work of God's perfect act of love and capable of returning that love. We are as God wanted us to be created, and with God's help, we can end up what God destined for us to become. The fact that we are unlike any other being in the history of the world is not a matter of defect, but of great honor. Being created in the image and likeness of God and yet totally unique, we are able to reflect God to the world in a way no other creature can. There is something about each one of us—in the way we were created and what is asked of us—that is particularly our own.

How wonderfully amazing is that? God loves us so much that, not only did he make us a creation unto ourselves, but in doing so, he gifted us with a particular way to return that love that is fit for no other person. In simply being our true selves, doing nothing more than becoming the unique person that God created us to be, we give glory to God and follow our own particular path of holiness. That's it! We are not to imitate the lives of the saints or do what others define for us; our path to holiness is not made by scrupulously following the path of a holy person who has gone before us. What is asked of me may not be asked of you. What you are capable of may not be what I am capable of. Each and every one of us has been created differently, for God's own glory, and we each have our own path to follow.

I love Pope Francis's words in this regard. In his apostolic exhortation *Gaudete et Exsultate,* he writes, "We should not grow discouraged before examples of holiness that appear unattainable. There are some testimonies that may prove helpful and inspiring, but that we are not meant to copy, for that could even lead us astray from the one specific path that the Lord has in mind for us" (#11). St. Francis may be the holiest man to ever walk the face of the earth, but if you think that I'm going to strip naked and jump into a bush of thorny roses, you're crazy! I think that Angela of Foligno perfectly exemplified what it means to be humble for the sake of Christ, but if you think I'm going to wash a leper and then drink the water afterwards, you're crazy! These actions added to the holiness of these great saints, but they are not things that would give glory to God through me. In fact, as I live today, they might even make me *less* holy, causing me to complain, to act selfishly, and to grow angry with others. In following after Jesus in holiness, our goal is not to imitate others—effectively putting on a false self—but to do nothing more than to be truly ourselves as God created us.

But how are we to know who this is? After a life of giving in to delusions of grandeur, self-loathing, and projections of any number of false selves, many of us might be left wondering what "truly ourselves" even means. Without a foundation on which to build, the act of leaving behind our false selves runs the risk of leaving only a crumbled façade with nothing behind it. Nor is this ever a "once and done" task. As followers of Christ, we will always be working on repairing and revealing our true selves.

For St. Francis, this search for himself began and ended by asking the only one whose opinion mattered: Jesus. Rather than filling his head with the opinions of the world, getting bogged down by his own self-doubt, letting his successes fill up his ego, he went to God in prayer and asked the two most essential questions anyone could ask: "Who are you Lord, and who am I?" So simple and pure, and yet so powerful. In these words and the response that follows is everything that could ever matter. How we come to answer them will define everything.

In my case, these questions inevitably draw me to littleness. When I ask God, "Who are you Lord, and who am I?" the image that always returns to me is that of a child of God. My place is not off alone ruling my own kingdom, but as the beloved in the kingdom of my Father. Despite being a finite creature in the midst of an all-knowing, all-powerful, ever-present Being—an absolute *nothing* next to God, in every way dependent and with no reason to boast—I never feel insignificant or unwanted. I am God's child, chosen and adopted out of love, called to love and serve in his kingdom.

What could ever matter more than knowing this? Truly, everything else is straw. Everything else is the working of a false self, an ego that knows nothing of reality. It is why in his admonitions St. Francis writes, "As much as [one] is before God, that much he is and nothing more." Nothing in all of existence matters at all except what God thinks of us. What we say about ourselves, what others think of us, who we wish were are—these are all useless questions, false selves that keep us from who we truly are before God, and prevent us from following after Christ with our whole hearts. If we want to be his disciples, the only self we can bring is the one that he created and redeemed. Everything else, we must let go.

What Must I Do?

1. Are there times in your life that you project more confidence, proficiency, or skill than you actually possess? What is behind this lie that you tell others? How might your life be different if you were a bit more vulnerable with others?

2. What is something good about you that could have only come from God? Do you thank God for such blessings? Do you honor God by sharing it with others?

3. Take a moment to pray St. Francis' prayer: "Who are you Lord and who am I?" Strip yourself of all of labels, categories, attributes, and expectations placed upon you by others, and begin to see yourself as God sees you.

chapter two

Expectations

From that time on, Jesus began to show his disciples that he must go to Jerusalem and suffer greatly from the elders, the chief priests, and the scribes, and be killed and on the third day be raised. Then Peter took him aside and began to rebuke him, "God forbid, Lord! No such thing shall ever happen to you." He turned and said to Peter, "Get behind me, Satan! You are an obstacle to me. You are thinking not as God does, but as human beings do."

—MATTHEW 16:21-23

Growing up, I had a tendency to get derailed when things did not go as planned. At least, that's what my youth minister told me when I had a meltdown at one of our events. At the time, I was a student leader in the church youth group, responsible for planning Sunday night meetings, major events, retreats, and general youth group activities. With the event in question, I had been the only student involved with every stage of the process, and so I knew exactly how everything was supposed to go.

Let's just say that things did not go how they were supposed to go.

The music wasn't right. There were last minute changes to talks. There were behavioral issues from some of the teens that required disciplinary actions. We were immediately behind schedule. And of course, it wouldn't be a major event if technological issues didn't make the whole team look like we had no idea what we were doing.

With every minute that went by, I got more and more frustrated. At first I was annoyed, then I was angry, but by the end of the first day I was just deflated and wanted to give up. *This is a disaster. What a failure.* All I wanted to do was quit and go home.

It was at this point that my youth minister sat me down and had a rather stern intervention with me. The event was fine, he said. Only a few people truly knew what was "supposed" to happen and the rest of the people were actually having a great time. In fact, it was *only* me that was unable to see how great the event was. In what turned out to be one of the most important admonishments of my life, he pointed out that I had a tendency to get stuck in a rigid mindset and be held hostage by my own expectations. Time and again, I had let the smallest changes to the plan ruin my experience and had failed to see the great things right in front of me. Like a train with an obstacle on the track, I did not adapt well, and the smallest debris in my way was enough to derail me.

I don't think we thank God enough for those people in our lives who are willing to speak the truth to us. He was absolutely right. When I thought through what I perceived as the failures of my life, I saw a consistent pattern: I would set precise expectations for the way something was supposed to go, minor problems would present me with a different reality, and I would become too frustrated with the disappointment to work with what I had. Great things were in front of me, but all I could focus on were my unrealized expectations.

Unfortunately, this problem is not unique to me, nor is it one that a life in Christ will protect us from. Despite knowing from the onset that following Christ means two sure things—God is ultimately in charge, and nothing we can say or do will prevent God's plan from being successful in the end—some part of us still resembles Peter rebuking Jesus. We have certain expectations, even certain *demands*, for the way things should go. Sometimes, even when we know these two constants, we find ourselves on the road to the kingdom but instead of being filled with joy, we're frustrated and disappointed.

Often we discover that our hopes are not of the kingdom at all, but of our own creations and fantasies. If we want to follow Jesus, we must let go of our hopes and expectations, our visions for the future, our demands for the present, and remain radically open to what God is doing right in front of us.

Narrow Visions

There is a reason that God forbade idols among his people, even when those idols were not of other gods: Images, by their very nature, are limited and subjective. When worshiping a God who is beyond time and space, immaterial and unknowable, any attempt to depict God would ultimately limit God. Images of God narrow our vision of the infinite into something totally finite. They are an attempt to contain what cannot be contained. To depict God as a warrior, wise old man, loving mother, or just judge can reveal a truth about God, but never the whole vision. In allowing ourselves to become fixated on a single aspect of who God is, we take what is not the fullness of God's being and call it God. That—a narrow vision of the transcendent—is precisely what an idol is.

While it is probably rare for people these days to construct physical idols of God (or false gods) in the way that the Israelites of the Old Testament did, we are not without our own practices of idolatry, limiting the scope of the kingdom and diminishing Christ's mission on earth. This begins with a narrow vision of *who* is included.

While the Catholic Church does not shy away from assuring the world of the presence of certain holy people in heaven—the saints— it might surprise many to know that it has not once made the reverse claim, officially assuring the world of a person's condemnation. As far as the Church is concerned, it is entirely possible that hell has no inhabitants at all. This is not a claim for universal salvation, that God necessarily saves all, but rather a careful attempt not to limit what God is capable of. Truly, we do not know the extent of God's mercy, and it makes us look rather foolish when we act like we do.

Oh, and we do. All the time.

Throughout the history of Christianity, those who called themselves followers of Christ were all too familiar with condemnations, exclusions, and outright hatred of those whom Christ wanted to include. How disgusting it is to see Christians harboring prejudicial feelings toward people of other races or ethnicities and excluding them from common life! How appalling it is to see followers of Christ, those who claim to be citizens of a kingdom not our own, blindly aligning themselves with a particular nation and rabidly attacking immigrants! Those who understand the vastness of God's mercy and the universal call of Jesus to all peoples are left dumbfounded when an organization like the Ku Klux Klan rises to prominence with a belief that racism and nationalism are compatible with the mission of the kingdom. Such structural acts of hatred have no place in Christ, and anyone who tries to wed them to Christ's mission makes an idol out of God: They do not worship the living and true God, but a limited fabrication used for their own power. As they say, "You know you've created God in your own image when he hates all the same people you do."

But let us not think that just because we do not wear white sheets and burn crosses on people's lawns that we are free of this idolatry. Any time we choose for ourselves who is not fit for the kingdom we find ourselves with a limited vision of that kingdom. We might not harbor an overtly racist attitude that seeks to inflict harm on others, but maybe we live with the subtle racism of low expectations, not believing that someone of a particular race or ethnic group is as capable as another. Maybe our problem is not with the color of one's skin, but with people we perceive lacking intelligence, work ethic, or usefulness, and so we refuse to trust them with important tasks. Maybe we are uncomfortable around those who are poor or resent those who are rich, and so we fail to welcome them into our churches. Or maybe we just have a strong sense of moral superiority, judging others' sins while failing to see our own, and we simply find certain people too far gone to be saved. In so many ways with so many people, we choose for ourselves who is capable of doing God's work and worthy of the kingdom. In doing so, we exclude some from the life of the Church; we fail to see them as a potential source of wisdom and life. In some cases, we even outright condemn them. When we do this, we fall into the idolatry of our own vision of the kingdom, limiting God's ability to work in our midst.

We don't need to search very hard in the Bible to see that God never chooses the ones we would choose, that God always surprises people by performing extraordinary tasks through the weak and lowly, the lost, and forgotten. Abraham was not a king, but a nomadic shepherd; Ruth was a Moabite woman, a foreigner; David was the youngest of eight sons from an insignificant town; Mary Magdalene had seven demons cast out of her. When Jesus took on human flesh, he was not born to a noble throne. He did not choose the most learned or religious to complete his mission. No, he spent his time with tax collectors and prostitutes, commissioned fisherman and shepherds, and even gave his life to the sinful and ritually unclean. When he dined with the rich and powerful, he called them to see beyond their social status.

Sadly, the Pharisees could not accept this. Their expectations for the coming messiah did not match the reality in front of them, and just like me in high school, they could not adapt. They became derailed. Truly, they became *unhinged*, filled with anger at the immense mercy that was before them, the unfathomably wide vision of God's kingdom, that they attacked the very God they thought they were protecting. They preferred their own narrow vision. They wanted a smaller, more containable God, one who loved the people they loved and hated the people they hated. They worshipped an idol.

How will we react when Jesus chooses to exalt the homeless person downtown, giving him immense wisdom that reveals to us that we actually know very little about life? What will we do when that woman we cannot stand, the one who made our life miserable for so long, is waiting for us next to Jesus, glorified in the kingdom of heaven? Being a disciple of Christ means abandoning our desire to choose who sits next to us at church, who is loved and forgiven, who God chooses to entrust with important tasks, and ultimately, who we spend eternity with. If the mission of Christ is like a dinner party in which we wait to respond to our invitation until we ask, "Who else is going to be there?" we might not be ready to follow him. When we place limits on who can enter and who God can use, we place limits on God and make an idol out of our faith.

The same can be said when we place limits on what that kingdom looks like and what is asked of us. One of my favorite Old Testament stories is the healing of Naaman in 2 Kings. Plagued with leprosy, he goes to the prophet Elisha for healing, expecting something amazing, but is disappointed when all he is told to do is wash in the dirty water of the river Jordan. Recognizing the dashed expectations in Naaman, his servants respond, "My father, if the prophet told you to do something extraordinary, would you not do it? All the more since he told you, 'Wash, and be clean'?" (2 Kings 5:13). In other words, just because it appears ordinary doesn't mean it is any less miraculous or effective. Let go of your expectations and rejoice in the fact that the Lord is healing you!

So often when we have a serious conversion to the Gospel, we feel that we must do something extraordinary. We look to the martyrs, the founders of religious orders, those who revolutionized the world for Christ, and we think, *now that I'm taking my faith seriously, I must do something like that.* And maybe that is precisely what Christ is asking of you; dream big, and let Christ change the world through you.

But maybe not. Maybe you will be asked to do something simple and mundane, certifiably ordinary: take care of an aging family member, be kind to a lonely neighbor, show humility and patience in the face of persecution. How easy it would be for us to look at those things and feel disappointed. *No, Lord, I want to do something* important *for the kingdom. I want to go to battle for you!* Looking to the heroism of the frontlines, we can sometimes forget that any good army needs accountants as well. Someone needs to keep watch at the base, send out important transmissions, stock the shelves. They may not be the valorous positions we dream of fulfilling, but they are no less integral to the success of the mission. As much as the Church needs the heroic, it also needs the compassionate, the steadfast, the prayerful, and those who are willing to hold down the fort for those who cannot take care of themselves. Sometimes, what is needed for the mission of Christ will not land us on the front page, and that may be disappointing, but our work for the kingdom is no less important. Like Naaman, what if something ordinary and mundane—taking care of an aging family member, being kind to a lonely neighbor, showing humility and patience in the face of persecution—was all that was asked of us to enter the kingdom of heaven? Would we not do it with great joy? We cannot let our own expectations of our place in the kingdom get in the way of what we are actually asked to do.

As a newly ordained priest, I begin my life in ministry with many high expectations for what God will ask of me. I look forward to a long life of preaching the Gospel, caring for the poor, advocating for justice, celebrating the sacraments, working with young people to promote vocations, and everything I do for the sake of evangelization on social media. I certainly have a vision of what a successful life of ministry should look like. But maybe—and I hate even the thought of it—God wants me to do something else. What would happen if I developed a degenerative disease that left me completely blind, unable to read, drive, or serve on my own? What if the Church or Order were to face tremendous persecution and I were left unable to practice my faith openly? What if—truly the most nightmarish scenario—I were falsely accused of some form of misconduct, was unable to clear my name, and so removed from active ministry for the rest of my life? It goes without saying that none of these situations quite fit my expectations of ministry. They would all be overwhelmingly devastating, in fact.

But they would not mark the end of my life working for the kingdom.

As much as I may have my own expectations of what my role for Christ is, it is not up to me to decide. I hope and pray that he may use me as a priest, but maybe what he needs from me is a symbol of humility. Maybe my purpose is to serve as a sacrifice for others. Maybe my place is not on the frontlines but back at the base caring for and encouraging those going out to battle.

If we want to be disciples of Christ, we have to let go of all our expectations. It means letting go of our narrow visions of God, rigid limits on who can be a part of the mission, and personal hopes for what we will accomplish. We do not have the full picture, and we look like fools when we try to paint it ourselves. Let God be God, and remain open to every wonder the kingdom affords.

Lofty Demands

As Christians, we say a lot of lofty things that sound absolutely wonderful. We quote the lives the saints, calling ourselves humble servants of God willing to do whatever is asked of us. In the face of adversity, we remind others that Christ died for us on the cross, and so we must also take up our own crosses, "offering up" our pain and sorrows. In the end it is worth it, we say, for all that we want in return is our salvation, an eternity with God. "My God and my all." "Let go and let God." These are the words that guide us, we say.

How amazing it would be if this was truly how we lived!

Unfortunately, as we know too well, our hearts are often divided. As much as we would like to follow Jesus unreservedly, and while we may occasionally go beyond our comfort zones and do virtuous works for the sake of the kingdom, our lofty words are frequently accompanied by equally lofty *demands* of God. There are strings attached, competing values that distract us from completely giving ourselves over to true discipleship. We expect things in our lives— and we expect God will provide them—to such an extent that their absence calls into question our faith in God and our desire to remain disciples. We rarely express these expectations explicitly, as if they were terms and conditions of a contract, but we can recognize them in the anger we feel toward God when things do not go the way we had wished, the ease at which we fall away from the mission in the midst of struggles, and even the renunciation of faith in the face of loss. More than just optimistic hopes or misguided visions, these demands are serious ultimatums: Rather than, "Let go and let God," our mantra can sound more like, "Get me this, or I'm going."

In my own life, this has often been the case with my sense of personal success. While I have never seriously expected to be famous or have a significant impact on human history, I would be lying if

I said I did not have high ambitions for my life. I wholeheartedly believe that my actions actually do matter, that hard work translates to success, and that some level of acknowledgment for these things is deserved. Even in the simple case of personal conversion, I do not think it crazy to expect, over the course of a long period of time, that prayer, fasting, works of mercy, and a desire to follow God will make me a better person than I am today. Progress in life is something I *expect*.

But what if it doesn't come? What if my actions turn out to have seemingly little effect on the world, I experience nothing but failure, and am ridiculed for even trying? Surely, as Christians, we know that this is not only possible but probable. Maybe even *necessary*. At no point in the Gospel does Jesus tell us that if we follow him our lives will be filled with success or that people will like us for it. Quite the contrary, actually! We follow a man who came to share the love of God with the world through healing and forgiveness, but was rejected by the religious elite, betrayed by his closest friends, and murdered as a common criminal. This is not simply Jesus's fate many years ago, but ours today. "Take up your crosses daily," he tells us. While there is nothing wrong with *hoping* for success in our lives, our faith is destined for problems if it becomes an expectation we cannot live without. The road of discipleship is filled with failure; if we *demand* that our lives be successful, we won't make it very far.

The same is true for those who expect the world to be fair. Everyone, we firmly believe, should be treated equally and be judged not by inert qualities that they cannot change but by the actions they choose. This sense of justice seems so imbedded a notion in all of humanity that even children cry out when something is awry; we instinctually know when we are being treated differently from others, feeling that things should be different. Justice should be exact and swift, returning to everyone what is due based on what they need and deserve. Good things should happen to good people and bad things to bad people. Our actions must have consequences, otherwise there is no order to anything.

And yet, just as surely as children intuit a sense of fairness, so, too, are children taught from early on that the world most certainly is *not* fair. As much as we can hope for equity in our lives, and as necessary as it is for Christians to work for the justice of the kingdom on earth, we live in a fallen world of greed, envy, violence, and hatred. Certain people are going to selfishly use their power to the detriment of others; certain people are going to exercise their God-given gift of free will for things entirely not of God's liking. Sure, God could take that gift back. God could intervene in every moment of our lives to ensure that everything is perfect in the world. But what would that make us? Without free choice, without true consequences for our actions, there is no freedom and there is no true love. Instead, as Jesus tells us in the parable of the wheat and the weeds, God shows his abundant mercy in allowing the bad to live next to the good for a while, but true justice will be exacted in the end. When we demand immediate justice of God, expecting that every moment of our lives be fair, we fail to see the larger picture of what God is doing and get in the way of the ultimate plan of salvation. This cannot be the case if we wish to be Christ's disciples.

As reasonable and understandable as any of these expectations may seem, following after Jesus with our whole hearts means that *any* demand of God is an unacceptable one. For what is a demand other than an assertion of power over another? When we demand something we approach another with a sense of entitlement and place upon them a nonnegotiable expectation that must be met if the relationship is to continue. *I deserve this from you.* Surely, this is not the way we want to approach God! If a desire in us gets to the point that our relationship with God is fundamentally dependent on a particular expectation, that we are so convinced of what we deserve that we are willing to make an assertion of power over God and place an ultimatum on our commitment to discipleship, clearly a part of us remains closed off to the fullness of God and is susceptible to falling away.

How sad it is to see major tragedies compounded by the loss of faith! Without realizing it, so many of us believe that a long and happy life is due to everyone. We *deserve* that. In fact, God has never promised us this. Almost every biblical figure experiences the tragedy of loss. And yet, when this expectation is not met—when children die, when loved ones are taken before we are ready, when natural disasters devastate countless lives—we can see it as injustice. When the lofty demands we never even realized we placed on God are left unmet, when what we believe we deserve has been taken away from us, our faith is shaken. *Why follow God if he won't give us what we deserve?*

But, really, what could we ever say we *deserve*? What right do we have to feel a sense of *entitlement* with God? Even in the case of natural and good things—life, happiness, safety, comfort—we must face the reality that we have done nothing to earn them. We stake no legitimate claim on them. The very fact that we have ever experienced them in the first place is not the result of who we are or what we've done, but a result of God's overwhelming goodness that gifts us with what we do not deserve. Thus, even in the absence of these things, *when we experience the tragedy of loss*, we have no right to stake a claim against God. What God gives, God can take away. We will naturally feel a whole range of emotions—anger, sadness, grief—and we may even express those feelings to God in prayer. But those feelings can't be rooted in a belief that God owes us anything.

Being a disciple of Christ means leaving behind anything we so expect that we bear a sense of entitlement. It means giving up what we think we deserve, what we say others owe us, and what demands we place on God. In doing so, we come to see everything in our lives for what it truly is: a gift. Only when we can see our lives as pure gift, as something that can be taken away without any anger or protest on our part, can we quote the words of the saints and actually mean them. Leave all your demands behind, and "Let go, and let God."

Cynicism

Of course, sometimes the problem our expectations pose to true discipleship is not that they are too narrow in scope or demanding in nature, but that they are entirely too bleak. Worse than distorted or unfounded hopes, some people simply cannot hope at all. *Nothing good can come of this. Things are the way they are and they are never going to change.* Left in the wake of too many disappointments and defeats, some people find themselves in a state of utter paralysis, only able to imagine the worst-case scenarios and resign themselves to low expectations. *What's the point of even trying?*

Unfortunately, a look to the world gives all-too-much fodder for this sort of thinking. It would seem that everywhere we look is scandal, disappointment, folly, or downright evil. The world appears to know no bounds when it comes to human depravity. Despite the appealing words of the most optimistic in our day claiming the triumphs of humanity and the steady progress of history, wars continue to rage on with no end in sight and poverty still claims the lives of millions while the few grow unnecessarily rich. Politicians lie to abuse their power, governments fall corrupt, and even the Church, which is supposed to be the shining light of Christ on earth, routinely undermines its mission with grave sins committed by its leaders. For the cynical at heart, the evidence is staggering.

Even for those with a more optimistic outlook on the world, it is impossible not to be affected by it all. For many, this is expressed simply as emotional detachment. The first time we experienced something horrific we react with outrage, devastation, and shock. *How could this happen? My entire world is changed!* Over time, with each new experience, what once seemed horrific begins to feel normal, as if it is the natural order of things, and we find there is no more outrage, devastation, or shock left to share. In many cases, we don't even notice it anymore. School shootings, terrorist attacks on foreign nations, thousands of human lives aborted, inmates executed—things that once shook our Christian souls to the core barely grab our attention. *It happened again. What a shame. I guess that's the world we live in.* As we slowly become numb to the reality, cynicism begins to grow in us. So commonplace, it is difficult to hope for anything else.

When this happens, it's only a matter of time before the cynicism of our low expectations creeps into our relationships with others. Think about what we teach our children: "Don't talk to strangers." Why? Because the world cannot be trusted. People want to take you, to hurt you. As we grow older and venture out we realize that this is not entirely the case, but it only takes a few examples of being hurt for us to revert back to childhood warnings. Maybe we experience a friend lying to us, a romantic partner cheating on us. Maybe we invest ourselves in someone we really love only to have him or her fail to reciprocate that love and eventually leave us. As these things occur with any frequency, we find ourselves more and more hesitant to put ourselves out there, less likely to engage people with much hope for any serious interactions, and possibly even begin to believe that it's not worth being vulnerable with anyone. *Look what happens when I let my guard down. I'm not going to let someone hurt me like that again.* Our expectations of others become so low that we are left unable to imagine anything but a worst-case scenario, and we act accordingly. Soon enough, it becomes easier just to stick to the friends we have, never venturing far from superficial topics and always maintaining a safe distance from others. Without high hopes for anyone else, cynical of what is outside, all that's left is to take refuge in ourselves, slowly slipping into isolation. *The only one I can trust is myself.*

Until our cynicism takes over that as well.

With so much distrust of the world and human nature, how long will it be until we treat ourselves with the same disdain? How long until we slip into self-loathing and defeatism. *I'm only human, you know! I am the way I am, and I can't change.* If our worldview is so defined by low expectations, if everything we do is so devoid of hope, it's simply impossible to believe we will be any different. With every personal failure, with every recurring sin, our ability to separate from what we've done becomes all the more difficult. No longer are we good creations of God that fall to sin. No, at some point it is much easier to see ourselves as someone who sins and cannot do anything to overcome our sins; at some point it is much easier to see ourselves as failures, useless and depraved, incapable of ever amounting to anything or accomplishing anything meaningful for the kingdom. *I've let God and myself down so many times, and I'll continue to do so. There's no way that God could use me.* With a cynical eye, all we can ever see is human limitation.

This is a major roadblock in our discipleship of Christ.

When we allow ourselves to be defeated, when we believe that nothing good can come of the world, when we give up even trying, we not only fail to see an entire history of amazing acts of heroism, selflessness, ingenuity, and progress exhibited throughout human history, we deny the very work of the Holy Spirit animating everything in existence. If we say that nothing good can come from the world, are we saying that the Holy Spirit is powerless or indifferent? Are we not putting our own weaknesses before the perfection of God?

The Good News of Jesus Christ is precisely that things *have* changed and that they are going to change even more. He came to a world that was stuck, to a people that could not find a way out of their sinfulness, to announce that there was *another* way. Better yet, he came not simply to announce this path and carry us there as passive recipients of grace, but empowered his followers to bring about the kingdom of which he spoke. The kingdom of God is *at hand*. It is not simply a far distant reality, but something that is inbreaking here and now, something that can be felt and brought about by those who live in communion with him. In the way we love one another, work for justice, and offer sacrifice—doing as Jesus did—we can *actually* make a difference in our world because it is in these moments that Christ dwells in us and the Holy Spirit is sent forth from us. What is it that we always pray? "Send down your Spirit and renew the face of the earth!"

If we want to follow after Jesus, we must let go of our cynicism and bleak outlook on the world, and instead believe with all our hearts that Christ is in control of this mission. We must look beyond what is not yet redeemed and open our eyes to the overflowing torrent that is God's love in our world, transforming and renewing the face of the earth. We must realize it is through us, those whom Jesus has called as his disciples, that this work is being accomplished.

Radically Open

I find it amazing how stifled our imaginations can be sometimes. We claim to believe in a God who is omnipotent, omniscient, ever-present, and ever-near, capable of doing anything imaginable, and yet we can hardly imagine much beyond our own finite experiences. So often, we place laughably small limits on what God can do, preferring a God and a kingdom of heaven that more closely resembles our own than the furthest reaches of our dreams; so often, we can barely expect what is beyond our own noses. It's no wonder, then, that we must often speak of a "God of surprises."

As long as I live, I will never forget one such surprise in my life. It happened during my fifth year as a friar, as I was going on my internship year in preparation for solemn vows. Knowing how important the ability to speak Spanish is for priests in the United States, and wishing to have a humbling experience of minority prior to taking vows, I approached my director of formation about spending the summer in Latin America to learn Spanish. Unbeknownst to me, another friar in formation happened to be within earshot when I asked and immediately jumped in, "Oh, I want to go too!"

My heart sank.

While the friars work to present the appearance of an easy-going fraternity of men who are of one mind and heart, loving and supporting one another like best friends, this is an absolute fantasy. As much as we try to get along, certain brothers just don't like each other. That's life, and that was my relationship at the time with this particular brother. Living together twice at different stages of our formation, we had rarely been forced to interact with one another, and I honestly cannot tell you if I had ever had a personal conversation with him to this point. Based on his personality and how he interacted with others, I had decided that we had little in common. Some of the opinions he had expressed were quite contrary to mine, and I assumed that the main reason we had never become friendly was because he did not like me. Of all the friars in formation at the time, I'm not sure that I could have chosen a worse companion for a grueling two-month stay in a foreign country. This was going to be a disaster.

It's funny how God works sometimes. Resigning myself to low expectations, writing this friar off as a problem, and limiting what was possible with God, I began the summer looking forward to the day it would end; when that day ultimately came, I found myself with a brother whom I truly loved and cared for. Taken out of our normal routines and forced to be together, surrounded by chaos and made to feel like we only had each other to trust in, we both rose to the occasion. When I was in pain as a result of some unfortunate medical issues, I saw a side of him that I had never experienced—patient, kind, and showing genuine care toward me. When he got stressed or angry, even at me, I listened to his complaints without fighting and offered as encouraging of a voice as I could muster. Over the course of two months, we shared our stories, aired our grievances, and dreamt together about the future. Entering the summer treating one another as little more than enemies, we came out the other side with what noticeably astounded us both: a new brother in Christ.

If God is capable of making me come to love and care for someone I had previously dreaded being around, truly anything is possible with God. The limits we place on the world, our Church, our loved ones, and even ourselves pale in comparison to what Jesus is leading us to on his mission.

Time and again, my little worldview is shaken by something wider; my plans are almost always dashed by bigger, better ones. If I've learned anything as a friar, it is that being a Christian means leaving behind absolutely everything I can imagine and being totally fine with accepting whatever God gives me—big or small, happy or painful. No matter what I come to expect, no matter how large and creative I think my imagination is, I always fall short of what God wants to accomplish. We cannot control the mission, and any attempt to cling to what we think we want only serves to slow down our own complete abandonment to Christ's leadership.

If we want to follow Christ, we must let go of every expectation or hope we may have because it will only serve to get in our way. We do not know where we're going, how to get there, what it will look like, or how long it will take. And that might seem daunting to us at first. But trusting in the fact that God loves us and wants the best for us, we can take solace in one thing: "eye has not seen, ear has not heard what God has in store for those who love him" (1 Corinthians 2:9)

What Must I Do?

1. Think of someone who is difficult to be around. Would it surprise you if God used them as a prophet to teach the world something? Is it possible that God is already doing this but you have refused to listen?

2. When was the last time that you got angry with God? What was behind the anger? In light of our call to live the Gospel without anything of our own, was this an appropriate thing to get angry about?

3. Take a moment in prayer to imagine the Kingdom of God. How different is it from our own world? What can you do—personally and with others—to bridge the gap?

chapter three

Anxiety

He said to his disciples, "Therefore I tell you, do not worry about your life and what you will eat, or about your body and what you will wear. For life is more than food and the body more than clothing. Notice the ravens: they do not sow or reap; they have neither storehouse nor barn, yet God feeds them. How much more important are you than birds! Can any of you by worrying add a moment to your life-span? If even the smallest things are beyond your control, why are you anxious about the rest? Notice how the flowers grow. They do not toil or spin. But I tell you, not even Solomon in all his splendor was dressed like one of them. If God so clothes the grass in the field that grows today and is thrown into the oven tomorrow, will he not much more provide for you, O you of little faith?

—Luke 12:22-24

When we were children, many of us were afraid of the dark. Whether it was lying in bed in an empty room or walking down the stairs to an unlit basement, there was something very unsettling about the dark. I distinctly remember the exhilarating fear of playing games like capture the flag or "ghost in the graveyard" when it was pitch black out, running around the neighborhood at night with only moonlight to guide us. My grandparents used to have a house in the mountains where there were no street lamps and woods all around us, and every summer my cousins and I would go out at night to play in the driveway or street, finding ourselves completely enveloped by darkness. When we were all together, it was extremely fun, even liberating. When we became separated or went our different ways to hide from whoever was "it," fear overshadowed us like the darkness. Every tree hid a potential danger. Every sound was something sneaking up on us. Without any light to see, we were cast into a world of unknowing—it was not the darkness that scared us, but what potentially hid in the darkness that gave us anxiety.

This, of course, is why anyone fears the dark at all, and truly what I think universally unsettles us from childhood to the end of our lives. The reason that children want nightlights is not because they are afraid of the dark *per se*, but because they want to be able to see what is *in* the dark. It is not so much the fear of the dark as it is a fear of being exposed, unprepared, and helpless in our surroundings. This feeling does not simply go away once we reach adulthood. While we may no longer fear monsters under the bed or walking down into a dark basement when we're home alone (at least, we're not willing to *admit* we are), there is something universally unnerving about not knowing or controlling our surroundings, of metaphorically being "in the dark." We want to see, we want to hear, we want to be in control. We make five-year plans, fill our calendars, chart spreadsheets and budgets, all so nothing will jump out of the dark and surprise us. We shine our nightlights on the future as brightly as we can so that nothing is beyond our sight. Most of us, I do believe, are still afraid of the "dark."

This can get in the way of complete discipleship.

As much as the idea of "eye has not seen" may sound inspirational to some and give all the more reason to abandon everything and follow Jesus, for many, there is something mildly terrifying about it all. We don't want to commit to things that our "eye has not seen"; we don't want to go where we cannot account for everything in our surroundings. Following Jesus offers us tremendous hope, yes, but it also means entering the darkness. It means letting go of our sight and control, turning off our nightlights, and trusting that he knows the way. Ultimately, it means leaving behind all that worries us and brings us fear, knowing that even in the dark, Jesus is the light of the world and protection from fear.

Need for Certainty

There is a strange infatuation in our world with being "sure." I would venture to say that the vast majority of us are looking for a "sure thing" in life. We tread the world cautiously, waiting to commit ourselves completely until we have some concrete proof. *Why believe in something unless we have absolute certainty?* In our time, it is seen as rational and prudent to think this way, to subject all knowledge to the scrutiny of the scientific method and to only believe that which can be proven empirically.

Interestingly enough, despite its overwhelming popularity today, this way of thinking is a fairly recent development in human thought—and not a very rational one. A result of the Enlightenment movement in eighteenth-century Europe, this sort of "logical positivist" thinking, as it is called, bears a major internal flaw: The idea that one can only believe that which can be proven empirically, cannot be proven empirically. In other words, science can give us answers to empirical questions, but science cannot give us a reason *why* or *how* we should study science in the first place, as its scope is limited to what can be deduced by mathematics and sense data. There is no indisputable reason to believe that the axiom has any truth in itself, and so this way of thinking fails its own criteria.

Surely there is more to believe in than what can be proven. How does one quantify beauty, goodness, or truth? How can science ever speak of an ethical way of life? What can mathematics ever assure us about love? When all we choose to believe is that which can be proven with certainty, we lose out on an entire world of meaning.

Unfortunately, this way of thinking has even crept its way into the realm of faith, and religious people find themselves committed to a bizarre and contradictory task of finding facts to prove their faith. There is an inordinate emphasis in many Christians to go beyond belief and to find surety. We see this in the often sensational and ridiculous television documentaries searching for the archaeological evidence of mythological biblical events, analyzing sacred objects for DNA evidence, and all of the "scientific" tests that do more mental gymnastics than anything else. But the problem is often found close to home as well. There is in our religion—and probably always has been—an infatuation with miracles and the regular revelations of so-called "visionaries," examples of revelation that can be anticipated, sensed, measured, and even "proved." *Who can dispute this miraculous event? Who can contradict what this holy person has seen? God* must *be real!*

On the surface, attention to these things may seem quite faithful, and many may interpret my hesitancy toward them as harshly critical, if not blasphemous. *How can you call someone's faith in miracles a bad thing?* To be clear, this is not what I wish to do; some miracles and visionaries are in fact authentic, as God has always used extraordinary means to speak to us. The problem, as I see it, is when people seek out miracles or visionaries, not as a *gift* from God to strengthen one's faith, but as a *replacement* of faith. Too often, the reason people are attracted to the extraordinary is because they are so plagued by overwhelming doubts that they cannot believe. They seek certainty in their faith, but this is a self-contradictory concept that can never be achieved.

Faith, by its very nature, cannot be proven. As soon as something has mathematical certainty—as soon as something can be sensed, measured, and recreated without any doubt or discrepancy—we no longer have a choice in believing. What is before us is a fact whether we accept it or not. This is not what God wants of us. If God's existence could be mathematically proven beyond any doubt (something that philosophical proofs like those of Anselm and Aquinas do not do) there would be no free will in our acceptance of God and so no true love in our following after Christ. As much as we may want to find that which takes away every ounce of doubt from our faiths, knowing with certainty that God exists, doing so would actually take away our faith as well. When we spend an inordinate amount of time focused on miracles and visionaries, we act not as those with faith, but as those who fear their doubts.

There is an even more fundamental problem at hand: I'm not sure that it is even *possible* for God's existence to be proven beyond doubt. Truly. Whenever I meet someone who is completely infatuated with extraordinary events, or when I encounter people wondering why God "doesn't reveal himself to the world now that there are cameras to prove that he exists," I always pose a simple question: what could God do that would give you the *certainty* that you're looking for?" Generally, they desire some extraordinary show of power, something beyond the physical laws of nature, including some booming voice saying something like, "I'm God, believe in me." Sure. Except, who's to say that what we'd be seeing and hearing isn't a hallucination on our part? How can we be sure that it's not the devil trying to trick us? Maybe it's all a dream and everything we're seeing is a projection of someone else's consciousness. The fact of the matter is that miracles and visionaries, no matter how impressive, cannot take away every shred of doubt and force everyone to believe. Pharaoh hardened his heart with every plague. The Pharisees claimed that Jesus was possessed by the devil. Hundreds of Jesus's followers deserted him after the bread of life discourse. Even in the face of the extraordinary, even when God has made God's presence clearly known, it is still up to us whether or not to believe what we've seen. Faith is a gift and it is a choice, but it can never be a certainty.

When we continue to pursue something that is impossible, we get stuck. Or worse, we actually *lose* our faith. I've seen it so many times. Applying the flawed logic of positivism to our faith, expecting to find proof for something when no proof can be found, faith is ultimately devastated. On the one hand, there are those who are so mired by their doubts that they will stop at nothing to find solace, uncritically accepting anything that supports a belief in God, no matter how illogical or strange it may seem. They want so badly to have proof that they are willing to see it everywhere, twisting their own sense of reason to fit square pegs in round holes, building for themselves a faith resembling a house of cards. Eventually, like every house of cards, it will come crashing down when one of the "proofs" that they cling to so tightly is taken away.

On the other extreme are those for whom no evidence is ever enough, and the constant disappointment of living in doubt is too much to handle. Held to such an impossible standard of knowledge, the lack of irrefutable proof may cause them to doubt the existence of God, but may seep into other parts of their lives. *How do I know I'm doing the right thing? Can I really know that my parents love me?* I once had a friend so overwhelmed with his inability to prove the important things in life that he began questioning our own existence. He could not be sure that the person talking to him—even himself at times—was anything more than a projection. *Maybe everything was in my head*, he often worried. *Maybe this is all just a hallucination.* I don't need to tell you this is a precarious place to be. In either case, as well as in far less extreme cases, the issue comes down to a distorted understanding of the role of doubts in our faith. So often, looking to St. Thomas, we grow uncomfortable with the fact that we want to see in order to believe. *My faith is pitiful! Why do I have such doubts?* While I suspect that most Christians see doubts as a sign of a weak faith, nothing could be further from the truth. When our doubts are like my friend's and we begin to worry about our own existence, yes, that is a problem, but the mere fact that we are not certain about something that cannot be proven is a sign that we are human. In fact, a faith without any doubts is probably not a faith at all.

In many cases, doubt is simply a question. When our finite experience butts up against an infinite reality, when we attempt to fit into our brains what only God can fully understand, we are bound to be uncertain with all that is not immediately comprehensible. We come face-to-face with the unknown, taking a step into the darkness, and we are left to wonder many things. This is not always a comfortable experience. We do not like the darkness! We do not like having our narrow worldview challenged, and we most certainly do not like questions without precise answers. We want certainty, but no certainty can come when our questions are of God. Truly, how could God be contained? Rather, our questions of faith simply lead to more questions, which lead to more questions, which lead on to infinity. In any other situation, this might lead us to accept that there is no end and so give up. In the case of God, though, the very act of questioning is the answer. It is in *having* the questions, resting in the doubts that we have, and accepting that we will never know it all but we can ask more questions, that we enter the mystery of God and find our home.

In following Jesus, we will never have certainty. We will never know for sure where we are going or if we are on the right path.

There will be times, as has been the case with all of the saints, when we will not even be sure of God's presence in our lives. Being a disciple of Christ means leaving behind impossible burdens of truth, the need to be sure, and our fears of the unknown, and resting in the overwhelming mystery of God.

Trivial Worries

I'm sure I'm not alone in this, but the only time that I enjoy cleaning and work diligently at it is when I have a lot of work to be done that's stressing me out. When I have a deadline approaching, I'm sure to have a stroke of inspiration to move all of the furniture out of my room and mop the floor; when I have to make a serious decision, all of a sudden I feel it's appropriate to take all of the books out of my library, lay them all over my room, and rearrange them in a more efficient order. In the face of stress, I run to these trivial tasks because they offer me some semblance of being in control and distract me from the discomfort I feel with weightier tasks.

This is precisely how so many of us operate in our spiritual lives.

Staring into the face of the mystery of God and accepting perpetual lack of certainty can be a bit too disquieting for some. So many of us are just hardwired to be in control, and so when we encounter things that we cannot completely grasp—the Trinity, issues of life and death, moral dilemmas—we don't know what to do. Rather than sit in the discomfort of that mystery, accepting that there are things completely outside of our control and trusting in God, our restless hearts seek something to fill the void. Like a child that can't sit still, we fill our lives up with "stuff" that doesn't truly matter, obsessing over them and making them the ultimate task of our lives. We dare not slow down lest we have to deal with the uncertainty of life's major questions. Despite how trivial they are, we convince ourselves that they are in fact paramount to our happiness and deserve our utmost attention.

In the Western world, I can't think of a better example of this than work. Not productive work that instills virtue, serves our community, and builds up the kingdom—this sort of work is essential to true human development. When I speak of work as a trivial worry, I'm talking about the frenetic, compulsive things we do that don't accomplish much more than filling our time: checking emails every ten minutes, rearranging a perfectly functional office space, micromanaging employees with questions they've already answered, showing up to work on our day off because we "just wanted to check on something." I have a friend that simply cannot sit still. We'll be out with a handful of people sitting around a campfire and he'll be on his feet for two hours—grabbing new firewood and stoking the fire, yes, but also arranging the wood in precise order, whittling twigs, fixing out-of-place rocks, and a host of other entirely useless tasks. At this point, it is no longer about getting something done or accomplishing a task, it is about finding something to do so our restless hearts won't have to sit still. In these cases, work ceases to be anything other than a trivial worry to keep us busy.

Worse yet is when the distraction we seek has nothing to do with actual work and everything to do with the arbitrary praise we receive from it. As someone who spent twenty-one years in school, I am talking, of course, of grades. Truly, is there a more trivial thing to worry about in all of life? While they no doubt serve a purpose within academia, and I'm not suggesting that schools entirely abolish the system, the fact is they mean absolutely nothing outside of the academic world. They do not make our lives better or measure our worth. Heck, they don't even indicate how much we've actually learned. The day after graduation, unless you are planning on going to more school, *no one will ever ask for your grades again.* I was struck by this reality when I transferred seminaries a few years into my formation. Having spent three years obsessing over my grades, worrying whether I would get a B+ or A- and what each would do to my GPA, the transcript at my new seminary was completely wiped clean: every class I took was listed as "transfer credit," without a grade, and my GPA started over at 0. *Oh yeah* I thought. *None of this matters at all. These letters mean nothing in the grand scheme of life.* How I wish I would have had that attitude ten years earlier! For so many of us, all grades do is give us something to worry about, to obsess over, to brag about and lord over others. This is wasted time and wasted energy in a fantasy world.

Of course, if it is an escapist fantasy world we're looking for to worry about, there is plenty of that to go around outside of academia. For millions, it is the world of sports. Is there anything so utterly trivial that has as much control over our emotions as sports do? The way that people get invested in particular teams or players, the way that we cheer, scream, fight, and even cry depending on how "our" team does, is objectively bizarre. Friends of mine know that leading up to a big game, I will actually be anxious, and after a loss I will be in a bad mood; I have even lost sleep over the success or failure of "my" team. I have never met any of these players, I have no financial investment in the team, and their success in no way reflects on me as a person. And yet, I invest tremendous amounts of time and emotion into them.

Those with no interest in sports and find the amount we worry about them ridiculous should be slow to judge. The entertainment industry serves the same purpose for others. I had a friend once who used to watch all of the Hollywood TV shows and read gossip magazines, spending ridiculous amounts of time trying to enter into the lives of celebrities. Whether conscious of it or not, she lived vicariously through the celebrities she obsessed over, finding an escape from her own world by feeling closer to theirs. Other friends have found this same refuge in video games. From the simple investment of time, playing multiple hours a day, to the full-on emotional investment of dressing like certain characters and imagining themselves in a different reality, virtual worlds offer a positive opportunity to be free and imaginative, but also a dark escape from the real world in front of us. Some can spend hours at a time staring at a screen, going on adventures and performing heroic acts with their characters, and yet remain distant and afraid of the real challenges to their right or left.

Which leads us to think of the ultimate example of trivial worries in a virtual world, social media. Oh, how much we as a people worry about how many times a picture of ours gets a "like" or how many followers we have; how amazing it is that we spend so much time curating our image and checking for validation. Some go through great effort to get the most perfect picture but fail to enjoy the actual experience. Lest I give the impression that I'm being judgmental of others, let me make it clear that I struggle with each of these things. As much as I use social media for the purposes of evangelism and catechesis, trying to stay above the fray, I find it almost impossible at times to avoid my desire for validation and my distress over negative comments. Against my better judgment, I find myself arguing with people I do not know about things that do not matter, letting it completely ruin my day, and sometimes, even letting it affect my self image. *This is not real* I have to remind myself. *This is a fake world! Likes, followers, shares, subs—none of this matters!* And yet, we treat them all like they do. Social media offers us an escape, a chance to be who we really want to be rather than facing who we really are. In a virtual world, we can have control.

And so we worry about things that don't matter.

Following Christ does not mean that we have to give up our jobs, schools, love of sports and entertainment, playing video games, or our social media handles. At least, not necessarily. What it means is that we need to let go of everything that produces anxiety in us and takes up our time without any benefit to ourselves or the world; it means giving up the trivial worries that merely keep us busy, give us something to think about, offer an escape, or hide us from what really matters. Christ calls us to the here and now. He wants us to be present to people and things that actually make a difference. If we want to be his disciples, there is no time to waste living in a world that doesn't exist. The kingdom is at hand, and it's the only world we need.

Impatience

Is there a more challenging virtue for our culture than patience? We want what we want when we want it. I don't know if this has always been the case, but it is surely the case now that we are driven by immediate gratification and find waiting to be among the most painful acts of penance imaginable. This is the case for superficial things like receiving our Christmas presents—celebrating the holiday weeks before and then throwing away the tree on December 26—as well as for far weightier things like justice. Forget the trial, forget due process. We want things resolved immediately so that we can move on.

Unfortunately, things rarely happen when we actually want them to, and we are left in all walks of our lives impatient for change. How many times have we looked at the world and thought, *it's the 21st century and this is* still *a problem?* There is a natural expectation of progress, a sense that we are stronger and wiser than our ancestors, and so the ills of the past should be gone. *We* still *have people in slavery? Wars* still *rage on between nations? When will we finally get it right and put an end to poverty?* With every sight of what we believe should be long eradicated, there is a temptation in us to grow more inpatient, more irritable, and more anxious about the world.

Looking to the Church, the same story repeats itself. *We've been around for 2,000 years and we're* still *making the same mistakes?* It's one thing to look to the early middle ages and feel ashamed of the Church's scandals, reading with horror of the scandals, abuses of power, acts of terror, and outright debauchery; seeing the Church today continuing to cover up scandals, abuse power, and fight with itself is just disheartening. In some ways, we appear to be further from the kingdom of God than we were two millennia ago! Our impatience builds, and many are left tired of waiting: *What's the use of watching history play out the same way again? I'm going to another Church.*

Of course, if we find ourselves impatient with the outside world, there is a good chance that we will also look at ourselves through that same impatient lens. Most of us are likely not recent converts; this means we have all been Christians trying to follow after Jesus for many years. We can find ourselves immensely deflated by every sin. *How am I still struggling with the same old things?* Having attended Church much of our lives and heard the story of Jesus proclaimed countless times, we know the difference between right and wrong; we know what is required of discipleship with Jesus; we know what we must do (or not do) to make a difference in our lives. And yet, we don't do what we know we must. We all fall short. And I do mean *all.* I look at my life as a solemnly professed religious, as an ordained priest, and I can't believe that I still miss the mark by so much. *Shouldn't I be holier by now? When am I finally going to be the person I know I should be?* I grow impatient with my own personal conversion, and I'm sure you do as well. We want what we want *when* we want it.

When will we finally become the people we hope to be? When will the kingdom come?

Unfortunately, the answer is obvious and most ungratifying: All things will happen as they are supposed to whenever God so decides. What does Jesus say in Matthew? "Of that day and hour no one knows, neither the angels of heaven, nor the Son, but the Father alone" (Matthew 25:36). While not diminishing our free will and the ability that God legitimately gives us to shape the world—we *can* make a difference—I find it helpful to remind myself that God is the ultimate facilitator of all of history and that God is much better at this stuff than I am. I may have my conception of what is appropriate and when something needs to be done, but I have no idea what I'm doing. I don't see what God sees and I don't know what God knows.

As finite beings it's easy to look at human history or the life of the Church and feel that it is a very long time. For beings that mostly live fewer than a hundred years, a millennium seems like an absurd amount of time, and it can be easy to grow impatient. Of course, this is nothing to God. "With the Lord one day is like a thousand years and a thousand years like one day." For God, all we've experienced is but a drop in the bucket. I had a professor once conjecture an interesting thought in this regard. Looking to the history of the Church, he wondered what we would think of our time period now if Jesus did not return until the year 20,000. As far advanced as we feel now, in such a reality, would we not be nothing more than the early Church, groaning with the pains of growth and self-identity? Without the long view, it is difficult for us to see what role our time plays in the whole of history and easy to grow impatient with the world. I wonder if we might take the same approach with ourselves. Sure, we may have been a Christian for five, ten, maybe even thirty years, leaving us understandably impatient in our personal conversions. But who's to say that we won't live another five, ten, even thirty years more? We might expect ourselves to be a fully functioning Christian today without any sins, but maybe we're not ready for that.

Maybe we have five, ten, even thirty years left to work out our salvation. Maybe everything in our lives up until this point served to prepare us for the step we are about to take, and had we been offered this step long ago we would not have been ready. If we were able to view life from the end, able to see the whole picture as God does, there's a good chance that we would see our present frustration in a different light.

God is in charge, and what is necessary will happen when it is supposed to.

Does this mean that we should disengage and merely sit back as passive observers until it's all taken care of? Of course not. What I am suggesting is not that our labors are insignificant or that we can make no difference, but simply that it is not our place to worry about the big picture. We are, as a prayer dedicated to Oscar Romero suggests, "Prophets of a Future Not Our Own." The difference we make is fundamentally significant to the life of the kingdom, but as workers in the field, we will never see all that the master builder does; as ministers, we will never accomplish what the messiah does.

As disciples of Christ, those wishing to follow after him, we are left with a critical question: Do we *actually* believe that God is truly driving history, that God is completely in control of the coming of the kingdom and all that is good? If so, and since we clearly don't have the vision ourselves, then it might be time for us to let go of our impatience and needless worries. Being a disciple of Christ does not mean that we get to make the decisions or have power over our situations; it means that we trust that God does and are completely content to let go of all that brings us anxiety.

Be Still and Know

I believe we are naturally restless people. For whatever reason, we feel our lives are somehow incomplete as we experience them and we long to fill in what is missing. We anxiously grasp at the world, hoping that more stuff, more wealth, more power, and more acclaim will satisfy us. Despite the futility of the world, something tells us it will bring us ultimate rest, but it never does. The more we seek, the more we realize how unsatisfied we are.

I would argue, interestingly enough, that this is among the best arguments for the existence of God. As we continue to search unsuccessfully for what will bring us rest, the longing we feel only grows stronger within us. With every question we are drawn to a wider horizon, forced to see ourselves against the infinite backdrop of our lives. Despite the ever-deepening hole within us and the futility of the world, something within us drives us to keep seeking, makes us believe there is something out there that will ultimately fulfill us. We refuse to settle, refuse to find comfort, no matter how much we have, because something within us knows that we need more. Our very longing points to that which can fulfill us. How true were St. Augustine's words: Our souls are restless until they rest in God!

As disciples of Christ, we must give up our restless anxiety and trust in God.

That means first and foremost trusting what we know in our hearts, what yearns within. Despite our doubts, we also possess some faith that we cannot explain, brief moments of calm that offer us a taste of a kingdom far beyond our own. There is something deep down that finds solace in the story of the Gospel and is filled with joy in the presence of goodness. Like the pregnant Elizabeth upon meeting her cousin Mary, there is something that leaps inside us at the presence of Christ. This is more than just wishful thinking or projection; it is our very souls reaching out for our Creator. In moments of doubt, do not worry that this feeling cannot be proven or quantified, but simply rest in it. Trust your feelings. Be still, and know that God has created you and speaks to you in the depths of your heart.

If this is not enough, trust in the faith that has been passed down for millennia. Things that are false, things that are destructive, pass away, but that which is true remains. For thousands of years, people of faith worshipped God and maintained a tradition of faith; for two thousand of those years, that people existed as the Church, a people founded by Jesus himself and guided by the Holy Spirit. Despite scandals and wars, abuses and threats, division and persecution, the people of God have refused to be turned away. They staked their lives on what they have seen, passed down what they have heard, and stood by what they have known to be true. Despite the world, the Church prevails. In times of frenetic anxiety, do not worry about what cannot be seen, but simply remember the faith of our ancient mothers and fathers. Trust in their examples. Be still, and know that God founded and guides the Church.

If that still is not enough to calm your fears, trust, finally, in the power of love and truth you find in the world. While we are quite familiar with being disappointed by the worst we see in the world, we cannot deny the extraordinary heroism of which humanity is also capable. All around us, ordinary people are performing acts of sacrifice, giving up their own lives so that others may live. It is nearly impossible to look into the world and not see love overflowing at every turn. Science cannot explain it; logic doesn't understand it. And yet, love emanates more powerfully than any substance we can measure. Truth transcends any instrument or equation. In moments of pessimism, when we find ourselves impatient with the world, do not grow hopeless, but trust in the unexplainable love lived by so many. Trust the goodness you see. Be still, and know that God is the source of all that is Good, Beautiful, and True, and that all love exists because God wills it.

For a world fixated on proofs and certainty, following a God of mystery seems ludicrous. Giving up our will and assenting to another seems like we're following blindly and passively. It may seem as though we enter the darkness because we can't face the truth. But we know through faith that this couldn't be more wrong. We enter the darkness, letting go of our need to know and be in control, not because we wish to be blind, but because it is the only time when we can truly see. In leaving our anxiety and trusting in God, we enter into the source of all truth and allow ourselves to be led in a way that we could have never found by ourselves. We may not know where the road leads, and that might cause great concern in us. But for those who trust in God, simply knowing *who* is leading is all we need to know. Following Christ is not about knowing where we are going, but knowing who we are going with, and trusting that he knows the way.

When Christ is our leader, we have no reason to worry.

What Must I Do?

1. If you could ask God any question, what would you ask? What does this desire to know say about your faith, and how might your inability to answer this question actually strengthen your trust in God?

2. Think about how you spend your time on a regular day. Are there things that you do that serve only to fill the silence and keep you busy? Try to replace some of those tasks with a quiet moment of prayer.

3. Take a moment to read the following prayer, "Prophets of a Future Not Our Own." How are you planting seeds today that will reap fruit tomorrow?

Prophets of a Future Not Our Own

It helps, now and then, to step back and take a long view.
The kingdom is not only beyond our efforts,
it is even beyond our vision.
We accomplish in our lifetime only a tiny fraction of the
magnificent enterprise that is God's work.
Nothing we do is complete, which is a way of saying that the
Kingdom always lies beyond us.
No statement says all that could be said.
No prayer fully expresses our faith.
No confession brings perfection.
No pastoral visit brings wholeness.
No program accomplishes the Church's mission.
No set of goals and objectives includes everything.
This is what we are about.
We plant the seeds that one day will grow.
We water seeds already planted, knowing
that they hold future promise.
We lay foundations that will need further development.
We provide yeast that produces far beyond our capabilities.
We cannot do everything, and there is a sense of
liberation in realizing that.
This enables us to do something, and to do it very well.
It may be incomplete, but it is a beginning, a step along the way, an
opportunity for the Lord's grace to enter and do the rest.
We may never see the end results, but that is the difference between
the master builder and the worker.
We are workers, not master builders; ministers, not messiahs.
We are prophets of a future not our own.

chapter four

Comfort

Meanwhile the boat, already a few miles offshore, was being
tossed about by the waves, for the wind was against it. During
the fourth watch of the night, he came toward them, walking
on the sea. When the disciples saw him walking on the sea
they were terrified. "It is a ghost," they said, and they cried
out in fear. At once [Jesus] spoke to them, "Take courage, it
is I; do not be afraid. Peter said to him in reply, "Lord, if it is
you, command me to come to you on the water." He said,
"Come." Peter got out of the boat and began to walk on the
water toward Jesus.

—MATTHEW 14:24-29

Before I entered religious life, I was pretty happy and most
certainly comfortable. I spent a lot of time with friends, had
a girlfriend I loved, and lived without much responsibility.
What could be better than college, right? While my specific situation
had to end—none of us can stay twenty-two for the rest of our
lives—I could have continued on that trajectory. My life did not
need to change much. After college, I could have found a job near
home, working to support myself but also marrying someone I loved,
hanging out with friends, and living in a familiar situation. I could
have stayed in the safety and comfort of the boat, easing down the
stream of life, and no one would have been the wiser.

But Jesus didn't want me to stay in the boat. He called me—like
he called Peter—to let go of the comfort of the familiar, the stable,

the "easy"; he showed me a different path and called me to walk out onto the water. What stood before me seemed scary at first, even impossible. I would have more readily stepped out onto a literal sea than taken a vow of chastity. *Why, when I've found something so safe and comfortable, would I risk my happiness like that? Isn't that what we're all looking for in life?* It seemed crazy to throw something like that away. But I needed to. As much as I liked what I had, and as much as I knew that I could have served God from where I was, I also knew that Jesus was leading me to something that would be better for the kingdom of God—and for me. As happy as I could have been as a husband and father, he knew, as I do now, that life as a vowed religious and priest would bring me even greater fulfillment.

This would not have been possible had I stayed in the comfort of the boat.

Jesus is calling each and every one of us from the boats of our own comforts. Maybe, like me, Jesus is calling you from the comfort of a traditional family close to home to religious life. But maybe not. Maybe the comfort that you seek in the boat is actually your own independence and lack of commitment, and what Jesus is calling you step out onto are the waters of a traditional family, committing yourself to others. While each of our vocations is uniquely different and what is asked of me is likely not what will be asked of you, one thing is true for us all: True disciples of Christ never get comfortable in their seats. Rather than staying where it is safe, clinging to what is familiar, they recognize that the mission of Christ does not have walls or limits, and being a disciple is not a nine-to-five job. Whether it be for desire for pleasure, a response to fear, or simply the result of overwhelming apathy, any comfort that leaves us sitting in the boat when Jesus is standing out on the sea is a roadblock to discipleship.

Jesus is calling us, and we must be willing to let go of what keeps us from him.

Pleasure

"This is the good life." How often I have heard this said (or said it myself) while sitting on a beach, refreshing drink in my hand, watching the sun set without a care in the world. The sky aflame with colors slowly melting away, the cool breeze wafting in from above. In those moments, all of the senses are engaged, each trying to take in every bit of the moment. It can be euphoric. Away from work, away from stresses and responsibilities, surrounded by nothing but what is aesthetically pleasing and physically comforting; many would call this "heaven."

This is the logic of the world, and frankly, it's difficult to argue with it. How could we possibly say that rest is bad? What could be wrong with enjoying the beauty of God's creation? Given one reading of Scripture, it would not take too much of a stretch to convince many people that such a situation *is* in fact heaven: a place filled with only that which is good, without a fear or worry at all. *That sounds a lot like the heaven Jesus describes in the Gospels.* For many, the goal for us while alive is to find our own "little piece of heaven," those moments of bliss, of pure pleasure without harm or distress.

The good life is about *feeling* good.

And if a little of something is good, a lot of it must be great, right? Such is also the logic of the world, leading many to believe that the entire purpose of life is to remove anything and everything that brings us harm and fill it instead with as much pleasure as possible. For some people, the perfect life imaginable consists of being surrounded by the greatest of luxuries—our favorite foods, a big home (or two) overlooking a gorgeous view, the latest gadgets and most stylish clothes, the fanciest cars and most extravagant accommodations—all without ever having to work again. Because, really, what could be better than sleeping in whenever we want and traveling the world on a whim? Depending on our social preferences, this perfect world might include outrageously fun parties or serene experiences of the highest class, but the point is we would be able to seek after whatever it is that brings us pleasure. In a way, the "good life" for many is nothing more than living out a fantasy of luxury and excess: all we can imagine, all we would ever want, at our fingertips without any responsibility.

Of course, since such goals are far from attainable for most without a multi-platinum record deal or extended contract with the New York Yankees, most people have much more tempered dreams for their lives: The "good life" can be as simple as a fine bottle of wine on a regular basis, driving an entry-level luxury sedan with added features, maybe just being able to add guacamole to a burrito without having to think twice. In fact, the excess of certain aspects of our world can be a major turnoff for some. A life of luxury worthy of the tabloids might seem interesting in our fantasy worlds, but many recognize that such a life can be extremely shallow and unfulfilling, even damaging to ourselves and our relationships. No, for many, the "good life" is not about having anything in excess, but simply about enjoying the little pleasures of life and being thankful for what we have.

Life, as many would say, is about finding what makes you happy and doing that.

On the surface, this perspective might seem prudent, even admirable, compared to the excessive one. Found on bumper stickers and inspirational posters, the idea of "only do what makes you happy" comes across to many as wise advice to an often listless world caught in menial jobs with lackluster lives. *With such a short life, why waste time on anything that doesn't make you happy? Life is meant to be enjoyed, not endured, so don't spend it on things that you're not passionate about.* There is something obviously appealing about this philosophy of life.

It's self-indulgent hedonism, but appealing, for sure.

Can you imagine if we *actually* only ever did what made us happy? My guess is that we would not have any friends, a job, or anything meaningful in our lives. The pursuit of happiness as a primary goal is an absolutely ridiculous mindset for life, one that, when tested, turns out to be short-sighted and downright selfish. Regardless of how high our ambitions are, when our desire for comfort is what defines what we do and who we are, what we do is going to be resistant to all forms of sacrifice, and who we are is going to be isolated from any authentic experiences of God.

Not everything that is meaningful and important in life will bring us immediate happiness. In reality, very few things will. Most things worth having require enduring much discomfort along the way. *Oh how much I would love to sit on the couch all day and each cookies!* If all I was worried about was my immediate comfort, that might be what I'd do. Of course, I understand that being healthy is far more important than the immediacy of my physical desires, and so I watch what I eat and go to the gym. Putting my body through grueling exercises is most certainly *not* what I want to do. It brings me pain, and my body rejects every second of it. But I do it anyway because I recognize that there are certain things beneficial in life that can only be experienced after great sacrifice.

So it is with our families. So it is with our careers. So it is with our faith.

Doing only what makes us happy provides a fading emotion and short-lived comfort, but Christian life is not about fading emotions or short-lived comforts. If all that matters to us is being happy, we will ultimately develop a selfish heart that is resistant to sacrifice and will struggle to find meaning in the cross. Personal happiness is simply not congruent with the selfless love of the cross. When there is no room for denying oneself, there is no room for the needs of others, and worse yet, no room for God. When this happens, God becomes nothing more than our personal giver and encourager, the eternal Santa Claus who answers our prays. Because we offer nothing of ourselves but seek only what brings us pleasure, our worship devolves into nothing more than the self-indulgence of enjoying a sunset: We receive beauty without having to give anything in return or be accountable to anyone else. When such is the case, we may *encounter* Beauty, but we will never fully *appreciate* it.

Not without selfless love.

Thus, being a following of Christ necessarily means enduring what makes us uncomfortable out of love. Jesus tells his disciples that they will be persecuted because of his name, that following him means taking up their own crosses. Historically, we know that many of the early Christians were greatly harmed because of their faith, and throughout the centuries we can see how those who stood up for the peace and justice of the Gospel experienced tremendous discomfort. In a less extreme sense, we know that there are certain things that we often desire that are against a good moral life. Whether it be food or drink, sex or power, seeking after them might bring us immediate comfort but no lasting satisfaction. It is only through conscious self-denial, often enduring some level of discomfort, that we are able to experience something far more meaningful than could have been achieved by indulging our initial desire.

So it is with our discipleship. Following Jesus does not mean that we will be comfortable or that we will be happy at every step along the way. In fact, my guess is that it guarantees we won't. The first disciples did not sleep at four-star hotels on the road to Jerusalem, and they were not always welcomed by encouraging crowds carrying their favorite foods. Life for a disciple can be difficult. But I can tell you, it was worth it to all of them, and to the Church. If we are unwilling to sacrifice what brings us pleasure, sometimes even leaving behind good and holy things that bring us happiness for a greater task, we will be unfit for the journey.

Fear

At the time I am writing this, I am at the age when many of my friends and family members are getting married. In many ways, it is a truly joyous time. Besides the fact that two people in love are making a tremendous commitment to one another, I get to see loads of people I enjoy being around for a catered event with an open bar. *Talk about a perfect combination!* That is, except for the dancing. I absolutely abhor dance floors and rarely step foot on them. When the music starts, I hang out to the side, mingle with those in their seats, and try not to be seen by anyone on the dance floor that might try to pull me out to dance. I just don't dance. Part of me will say that it's because I simply don't like loud music and tons of people, but that's not entirely true. Another part says that it's because I don't have anyone to dance with (and because a priest really shouldn't be in such an environment), but really, there are plenty of opportunities to have a good, wholesome time on the dance floor among a group. No, when I'm entirely honest with myself and ask why I avoid dancing like the plague, I see a different reason: Deep down, I'm afraid. Afraid of looking like a fool. Afraid of not knowing what to do. Afraid of being made fun of. As someone who values success and personal image as much as I do (yes, those false selves), I have spent my life avoiding things that I am not good at, and dancing is one of those things. Out of fear for what I might lose, I stay off to the side, preferring the comfort of the boat than the joyful potential of the waters.

I believe that this is the case for many people. The reason they take refuge in what is familiar and safe is not necessarily because they *like* these things or think that they are the most fulfilling parts of the human experience, but rather that they are too afraid of what they might lose if they take the risk. *Yeah there are so many cool things to do outside, but the world is such a dangerous place. I could get hurt!* When fear comes to rule our lives, influencing all that we want and all that we care about, comfort becomes our central goal. Rather than venturing out into the world and experiencing the magnificent wonder that God has created, rather than being vulnerable to what might surprise us and challenge us, we build walls to protect ourselves.

Sometimes these walls are physical structures, literal barriers to keep out all that we fear. Just as some nations erect fences with barbed wire in an attempt to keep out foreigners, we, private citizens, build brick-and-mortar houses to hide us from the outside world. There, within our mini fortresses, we can close our windows, lock our doors, and completely shut out our neighbors. We can erect fences and privacy barriers between our yards, security systems and hidden cameras at every corner. We may have no-soliciting signs on our doors or live in a gated community. In the comfort of our homes, we can be assured of our privacy, and this gives us a sense of being in control.

But it doesn't stop at our homes. In an attempt to keep unwanted people out of our lives, we seek refuge behind the comfort of our institutions. Country clubs and owners' associations require such steep fees and enforce such strict rules that one can easily surround oneself with the "right" type of person. Schools and universities selectively choose who to admit and how one must act on their premises. Even churches—once the literal "sanctuary" for fugitives—serve as hide-aways from the world, safe enclosures of the spiritual realm, keeping their members from the stresses of normal life. Many would think that my goal as a priest is primarily to get people *into* church, but the reality is that I spend just as much time trying to get people *out* of it. Far too many people spend their time at church because they fear the world; for some, church is not so much a source of strength so as to better *serve* one's neighbor as it is a place to *hide* from one's neighbor and the many problems of our world. Like other institutions, the Church can become a refuge of physical walls as a means of controlling what and whom we encounter. Out of fear, these barriers offer us comfort.

But as effective as physical walls can be in protecting our bodies, they do nothing to protect how we feel: For those with fears of a broken heart, many will resort to building emotional walls. Invisible and immaterial, they can be taken anywhere and are almost undetectable. Accompanied with a smile, surrounding the friendliest of people, emotional walls allow them to live in the world with the appearance that they are perfectly fine. Some might even be in long-term relationships. At least, part of them is. Emotionally, they remain distant and protected, almost never completely honest with their feelings and rarely trusting others. *You can't hurt me if I don't let you.* I once lived with a friar who never shared a single personal story. Not once. We talked about sports, politics, and the church; I shared my own personal stories and offered opportunities for the two of us to be vulnerable with each other. But never—not once over an entire year of living together and having countless conversations—did I ever hear anything about his time in college, past relationships, what he feared, what he loved, or a tragedy he faced. I spent hours upon hours with this friar, and I can truly say that I know almost nothing about him. For whatever reason, he never moved beyond the superficial, he never put his walls down far enough for me to see inside. The answer, of course, could be that is was simply *me* that he did not trust, that he was actually quite open with others, but I suspect that was not the case. The way he interacted with other friars, his shyness around parishioners, the amount of time he spent by himself all pointed to a man who was protecting himself. Sadly, he lived afraid of something and found refuge behind the walls he put up around his heart.

For others, fear stretches beyond physical and emotional boundaries into the most abstract and unidentified parts of ourselves: our intellects. While it is not uncommon to see people afraid of physical harm and emotionally distant, I'm not sure if either of these compare to the fear of ideas I see in so many places today. People are rabidly afraid of opinions different from their own and ideas that challenge their worldview. Look to the internet and you will find an increasing number of people entrenched in perspectives that are verifiably incorrect: "the earth is flat," "vaccinations cause autism," "climate change is a hoax," "Catholicism is a cult." It doesn't matter how much verifiable, irrefutable evidence they are shown, these people will never change their mind. They let their anchor down, dig into the mud, and place intellectual walls around themselves. *That's a lie. You don't know what you're talking about.* In our Church especially, I see people who are so convinced of something that they are more willing to dismiss new ideas as "modern" or "heretical" than listen to them thoughtfully. How often I try to teach someone something I know to be true—I can even show them the exact quote in the Bible or Catechism—and they will reject it. *That's not what I was taught.* The world, as they see it, is filled with cunning and deceitful people, and so it is safer to wall themselves off from it. They know what they know and don't need to get mixed up with anything new.

Out of fear, we build walls. All of us do, and honestly, it's completely understandable. Frankly, it's biological. Out of a primal instinct to protect ourselves from danger, we rest in the comfort of what is familiar, what is easy, what is safe. Our walls might be physical or social, emotional, or intellectual, but at times, we all find refuge in them. We all work to preserve what we have and do not want to lose.

Of course, there is an obvious downside to building walls: Just as effectively as they can keep dangers out, they can trap us in. When we put up walls, we do not simply block what causes us harm, we block what brings us joy as well. We enclose ourselves in a small world without the possibility of growing, changing, or being surprised. There is no sunlight or fresh air, no new inspirations or challenges, just a bunker full of ourselves. When this happens, it is only a matter of time before we become tremendously sick, so cut off from others and turned in on ourselves that we no longer care about the body of Christ, only our own bodies.

Fear is a sickness. Comfort can slowly stifle us.

How I love Pope Francis's words in *Evangelii Gaudium!* At the conclusion of his opening chapter, setting the work of transformational missionary action as the foundation of Christian life, he writes, "I prefer a Church which is bruised, hurting and dirty because it has been out on the streets, rather than a Church which is unhealthy from being confined and from clinging to its own security." What he desires from the Church is a people who are less concerned with their own comfort than with the mission of Christ, a people who are less defined by their fear than by their commitment to the Gospel, a people who are willing to take risks because there is something greater at work in the world than danger. This is the mission to which Christ calls us. And, yes, it might leave us bruised, hurting, and dirty at times, but what good is it to be healthy and safe if we have nothing—or nobody—to live for?

Choosing to follow Christ does not mean we will magically overcome our fears or live comfortably despite them. What it means is we will be able to acknowledge that our fears exist, and act anyway.

Apathy

Every year, new studies are released reporting the number of people in each denomination and religion in the United States. As of late, the trend has been bleak: People continue to walk away from organized religion. Leaders and pundits jump on these findings, using them as evidence to support whatever their argument is against the current state of the Church. *See what the LGBTQ community is doing to our Church! If only we ordained women this wouldn't be a problem! This is why we need to go back to the way things were!* In the case of dropping church attendance, many want to look to the problem through the lens of a particular hot-button issue, asserting that the reason people leave is because of a passionate disagreement with a certain aspect of the Church that needs changing. And there's certainly some truth to that. Some people *do* leave for conscious, intentional reasons. But most do not. In my experience, the vast majority of people who leave do so over a long period of time, without a specific reason, without a definitive departure, and sometimes without even realizing they've left. It's a slow fade. Because of one thing or another, they find excuses to do something else, and with no strong passion for Christ or the Church—nothing to overcome the regular busyness of life—they never return.

They leave not because they are hot or cold; they're simply lukewarm.

I suspect this is an issue for all of us from time to time, regardless of our church attendance. For most of us, the comfort that gets in the way of our discipleship is not the fire of hedonism nor the chill of fear. No, we cling to our comforts not out of passion or necessity, not with such strong resistance that we can hardly imagine living without them, but simply out of convention and convenience. The reason we stay in the boat and never venture out onto the waters with Jesus is because we're stuck in inertia. We slip into a rhythm, somewhat without even noticing, and never find a reason to get out. *I'm already sitting. Why would I stand up?*

So many are just spiritually apathetic.

At its best, one might describe this predicament as floating through life on a path of least resistance. *Why fight through life or make plans that are just going to get ruined anyway?* I had a friend once who "lived in the moment," as he would say, and never ventured beyond what was directly in front of him. He had no idea what he was going to do in life, and honestly, had no care about it either. He would get a temporary job, work for a bit, then move onto something else. After college he moved back with his parents, not because he was saving up for something bigger, not because he had plans for something better, but because it was what he had always known. He enjoyed the familiarity of his home, the comfort of his mother's cooking; he liked knowing where everything was in his surroundings. He did not live for pleasure, nor did he resort to this life out of fear, he simply didn't feel inspired enough by anything to take a step forward. What he had was comfortable, so why mess with it?

Unfortunately, his situation is not unique, nor is it particular to men in their twenties. All around I see people in careers they care nothing about, in relationships with people they no longer love, sticking to ideas for no other reason than, "That's the way it's always been done," even showing up to church and sleeping through services to fulfill some obligation. Their lives lack passion. They act not out of love or hate, not with intentionality or purpose, but simply out of a sense of familiarity. What they have may not be great, but it's comfortable, and that's good enough. They know they're in a rut but find great truth in the old adage, "The devil you know is better than the devil you don't." Things could be much worse. *The boat isn't sinking, so don't mess with it by trying to stand up.*

There's just one problem: known or not, it's still the devil.

I think apathy is the greatest asset of the devil. As easy as it is to see the folly of hedonism, blindly following one's passions for pleasure, and as lifeless as it is to be defined by one's fears, hiding from the world, each of these approaches is actually based on something that is good: However distorted in practice, pleasure and safety are essentially gifts from God. Burning with passion for these things distorts the gift, but at least there is *passion*. At least there is *life*. At least God has something to *work with*. Remember what God says in the book of Revelation: "I wish you were either cold or hot. So, because you are lukewarm, neither hot nor cold, I will spit you out of my mouth" (Revelation 3:16). When people are lukewarm, apathetic to things that truly matter, refusing to care or get involved in anything, there is little God can do to rouse them. I truly believe that God would rather us be committed sinners, passionately running after something distorted with conviction, than not running at all. I've said it before and I'll say it again: God can change our direction, but God cannot make us move. At best, being a slave to convention debilitates our ability to follow Christ.

Of course, it can be far worse.

Despite having little passion for anything worthwhile in life, one thing will rouse the spiritually apathetic to action: the threat of change. So attached to the status quo, so dependent on the comfort of the familiar, they cannot imagine life any other way. New ideas, even good ones, must be eliminated; agents of change, even for the better, must be belittled. How sad it is to see those so concerned with remaining unbothered that they will actually go out of their way to obstruct the work of those trying to make a change. Worse than simply being detached and unconcerned with the mission of Christ, some will go as far as to get in Christ's way in order to maintain their own comfort.

I think of the bureaucrat at any business who has done something the same way for thirty years and refuses to make a change, no matter how inefficient it might be to the customer or company. I think of the mother or father who, when his or her child expresses an interest in doing something creative or adventurous, shows disapproval and forces them to do what everyone else in the family does. I think of those who complained about the inconvenience of civil rights workers in the 1950s and 60s, those who were more concerned with the buses running on time than on the authentic human development of an entire ethnic group. *Why do they need to break the law? Think of the people who were late for work because of their protest. They should have more respect for others and stop causing such divisions.* In every age, there are those who place so much trust in the comfort of familiarity that they are willing to fight to protect it, no matter how unjust or unproductive the familiar actually is.

Apathy is far more than spiritual laziness. Sometimes, it can be downright evil.

Those who find themselves in such a state, clinging to what is familiar at the expense of what is right and just, would be wise to remember Mary's words in her Magnificat: "He has shown might with his arm, dispersed the arrogant of mind and heart. He has thrown down the rulers from their thrones but lifted up the lowly. The hungry he has filled with good things; the rich he has sent away empty" (Luke 1:53). All throughout her hymn—and frankly, all throughout the Gospel of Luke—we hear of a coming kingdom that will usher in great changes. Read the Beatitudes, the parable of the Rich Man and Lazarus, the parable of the Good Samaritan, and the comparison of the tax collector and the Pharisee. What Christ's life announces is that the world is about to be turned upside down. Being a part of his mission means accepting a reversal of fates. Those who sit comfortably on their thrones, unconcerned with the plight of the world? Beware.

We can walk with Jesus, whose mission will be accomplished whether we like it or not, or we can grasp at our fleeting comforts, getting in his way. It doesn't seem like much of a choice to me. If we want to follow after Jesus, we need to let go of our apathy and laziness, the comfort that comes from being disconnected from others, and begin to truly care. Discipleship is about a life of passion, about giving our lives completely over to the mission that Christ is calling us to. Either we're fully in, or we're not in at all.

God Seeks to Unsettle

It's no coincidence that the most meaningful encounters with God in the Bible happen when people are in the desert. Moses witnessed the burning bush and received his call; Elijah heard the "light, silent sound" of God speaking, offering him reassurance; even Jesus himself was led by the Spirit to be tempted in the desert. By definition, a desert is a place of complete desolation, absent of creature comforts and most likely unfamiliar to the average person. Few are at home in the desert, and that is precisely the point: in the desert, there are no pleasures, no means of safety, and nothing familiar from our everyday lives. We are exposed and vulnerable. Free of their worldly comforts, shaken up, and most certainly uncomfortable, there is nothing left to rely on but God.

This is *exactly* what God wants.

The most important people in my life have always been the ones who *unsettled* me. Not the ones who comforted me and told me I was special and everything would be okay. No. The ones who challenged my worldview and forced me to do things that I didn't want to do; the ones who stretched me and even said that they were disappointed in me. For as long as I live, I'll never forget an admonishment I got from a close friend who told me things about myself that I did not want to hear. Here I thought that I was doing pretty well for myself, saw myself as a pretty good guy. No one is perfect, but, you know…I had my life pretty well in order. In just a few words—said with love, but by no means comforting—he flipped the perception I had of myself completely upside down. He unsettled the neat little world I had created, the comfortable image I had of myself, and forced me out of my complacency. I had unwittingly sat down in the boat and gotten comfortable with my life. I needed to be unsettled.

While some of the bad things that happen in our lives result from evil in the world and some from our own poor decisions, we can often see the hand of God in some of the upheaval in our lives. We are called into the desert and stripped of our comforts, not for the sake of harm in itself, but because we have ignored the invitation to walk out onto the water for far too long. We're anchored in our seats, God can wait no longer, and so, a storm comes to throw us out. *If you won't come out willingly, I'll just have to capsize the boat!* As odd as it might sound to some, God is not concerned *primarily* with our happiness. God cares *nothing* of our comfort. All that God thinks and does and cares about is directed to our salvation, breathing life and love into us so that we may choose to return to the source of Life and Love. Sometimes, like a close friend admonishing us to awake us to our blindness, God unsettles us so we can attach ourselves to something that truly matters.

Let yourself be unsettled. Let God shake up your world. The longer we cling to the comfort of our seat in the boat—whether it be because of the pleasure, safety, or familiarity it offers us—the longer we will find ourselves away from the Lord. He is calling us out onto the water, and there is only one thing left to do: jump. There will be times when it is far from fun, positively dangerous, and even a bit lonely, but it is what we all must do. If we want to be disciples of Christ, we must get out of our seats and walk with him.

What Must I Do?

1. Sometimes, the Gospel is simply inconvenient. It requires sacrificing time we planned for ourselves for the sake of another. How do you react when faced with unexpected tasks, difficult people, or uncomfortable situations? Do you willingly let go of your comfort, or do you find excuses not to help?

2. Some have suggested that there are but nine root fears: personal corruption, rejection, failure, inadequacy, ignorance, abandonment, boredom, weakness, and conflict itself. Which fear is most prevalent in your life? How does this fear prevent you from giving your entire self to the mission of Christ?

3. Generally speaking, how do you respond to change? Reflect on the image of Jesus turning the world "upside down." Are you ready to be a part of that?

chapter five

Wounds

On hearing that it was Jesus of Nazareth, he began to cry out and say, "Jesus, son of David, have pity on me." And many rebuked him, telling him to be silent. But he kept calling out all the more, "Son of David, have pity on me." Jesus stopped and said, "Call him." So they called the blind man, saying to him, "Take courage; get up, he is calling you." He threw aside his cloak, sprang up, and came to Jesus. Jesus said to him in reply, "What do you want me to do for you?" The blind man replied to him, "Master, I want to see." Jesus told him, "Go your way; your faith has saved you." Immediately he received his sight and followed him on the way.

—MARK 10:47-52

When I was sixteen years old, I became a follower of Christ. I don't mean that I became a Christian—that happened when I was baptized as a child, sacramentally marked by Christ and so as authentically Christian as I will ever be. No, at sixteen, I consciously decided to be his disciple, to devote my life to imitating him and carrying out his mission. For years, like all kids, I attended mass because I was forced to; I called myself a Christian because that's what my parents chose for me; I believed in God, but really, just said my prayers because that's what I was "supposed to do." I was undoubtedly a part of the Church, but Jesus played a very small part of my actual life.

That all changed when I was sixteen.

There came a point when my entire disposition toward faith changed, when it was no longer imposed on my life by my parents, but an active choice of my own. There came a point when I believed for myself, and I wanted to follow Jesus in every aspect of my life. That point was on a high school retreat to the mountains. After a fun day of team-building games and light-hearted activities, I was handed a block of wood and a marker and told to write down anything and everything I experienced as a burden in life. There were no rules or right answers. No one was going to be checking what I wrote. Just sit in silence for a few minutes and be honest with ourselves. *What is weighing on me right now? What is getting in the way of a happy and free life?* However we understood the prompt and whatever we wanted to write went onto that block. We could write one big thing or we could fill up every inch of the block of wood with personal notes. And when we were finished writing, we were told to throw the wood into a bonfire.

I don't think I have to tell you how cathartic this sort of exercise can be. There before me was everything I found burdensome—my sins, pains, angers, regrets, jealousies, anxieties, fears—burning into nothing. Watching those words burst into flames and slowly disintegrate was intensely satisfying and undoubtedly healing. While I knew it was nothing more than a symbolic act, that none of these burdens were in any way affected by burning a piece of wood, that none of my sins were actually forgiven simply by writing them down, I found myself profoundly moved by what the ritual evoked: I came to understand there is no burden that Christ has not already carried and is able to completely obliterate. In Christ, our wounds are nothing more than dry wood in a fire.

It was in that moment I realized I wanted to devote my life to him.

Stories like mine are the most prevalent in the Gospels: Jesus gained followers by healing people of all that took life from them. He came not simply to preach of a future kingdom, but to remove all that prevented people from living fully today; he cared not just about souls, but about physical afflictions, emotional pains, moral wounds, and social alienations. In all matters of death and despair, Jesus brought life and hope. No wonder it is called the Good News!

No matter who we are or where we've been, we all bear the wounds of a fallen world, and Jesus wants to heal us of all that afflicts us. Unfortunately, many people are either unable or unwilling to believe this; unfortunately, many people do not accept Christ's desire to heal us. I do not believe we can fully follow after Jesus if we are unable to call to him for help and allow him to heal our wounds. If we wish to be his disciples, we must let go of the denial, self-pity, and despair that gets in the way and seek the one who can heal us of those burdens.

Denial

It might seem peculiar, given his mission of freely healing all whom he met, that Jesus asked the blind man what he wanted. *Wasn't it obvious a blind man would want to see?* If the purpose of Jesus's question was merely to determine the man's ailment, it might seem like a trivial question. But I don't think that's why Jesus posed it. The question was not for Jesus's benefit, but for the blind man's: He needed to admit his weakness, let go of his burdens, and be vulnerable enough to ask for help.

The biggest obstacle getting in the way of Jesus's healing touch is our own denial that we need help. How often in my life I have let my pride get in the way and refused the help I really needed! For fear of appearing weak or because I thought people would think less of me, I pretended I was fine when I was actually in the midst of a crisis. I think of the countless times in my life when I hid in the superficiality of small talk, responding simply "I'm okay" or even, "I'm great" when someone asked how I was doing, not wanting to burden others with my problems. I might have been having the worst day of my life, truly worried about something serious, and yet chose to put on a brave face as if nothing were wrong.

As a priest, I routinely speak with people who have carried burdens for years, even decades, without telling a single person. They sit down in my office or in the confessional and share how they have lived with crippling guilt their entire adult lives, how they struggle with a particular sin, how they were abused as a child, how they live in fear but have no idea what to do. As humbled as I am that they chose to confide in me after all of these years—truly one of the greatest gifts of being a priest—I can't help but feel sad for them: How many years, even decades, had they missed out on the healing they so desperately needed!

For some, the burden feels too difficult to admit to another person. We fear that if we are vulnerable, if we share the secret that has plagued us, we will be rejected and our problems will only become worse. *What if they laugh? What if they don't accept me?* Sitting before the fire with my block of wood, absolutely debilitated, this was my problem. While the burdens I was carrying were by no means life-threatening or dramatic enough to bother listing here, I found myself distinctly afraid to share them with another person. To this day, I will never forget how long I sat there, staring at my blank block of wood. It was as if I were frozen. All I had to do was write down words on a soon-to-be-burned block of wood, but I couldn't. I knew that in writing something down, I was forcing myself to admit, probably for the first time in my life, that I was wounded, that there were things inside of me that hurt and brought shame, that I needed help, and most of all, that I needed to let someone else help me. In writing something down, I was symbolically acknowledging that I needed to let go of past pains and begin to live in a radically different way. I found myself overwhelmed with emotion, shaken to my core. I sat there for almost an hour and could not write a single word. I cried to myself, and then with a friend. Although it was just a few words on a block of wood, I knew it meant so much more.

Sometimes, we carry our burdens privately because we are even afraid to acknowledge they exist. But we must! We must speak them and let them go. On my retreat, the fire might have been burning, but it didn't matter if I was unwilling to write anything down. As much as Jesus wants to take our burdens and free us from sin, he cannot do this unless we ask him, unless we are willing to admit to ourselves that something needs to change, and accept his help by changing our lives. For me, it was the act of writing on a block of wood—more than watching it burn—that changed me forever and made me into a disciple. It was in that act I learned to ask for help. Like the blind man, I was vulnerable and called out to Jesus, "Son of David, have pity on me!"

Rather than face what we fear, accepting that we need help, we deny our need for help, even to ourselves. At some point, we become so afraid of our wounds, so afraid of admitting we have a problem, that we hide our problems even from ourselves, engaging in mental gymnastics and reshaping the world so we can fit in as we are. We tell others we're fine, and we begin to believe it ourselves. We remain the walking wounded, trapped by sin and pain, yet ignorant of our situation.

This is a huge stumbling block on our spiritual journeys as disciples. As anyone who has ever tried to help another knows, no amount of effort on the part of the healer will make a difference if the other refuses to accept it. It doesn't matter if our issue is with

anger, depression, obesity, being late for meetings, personal relationships, addiction, or any form of sin, if we deny we have a problem, we
are never going to be able to overcome it.

We cannot call ourselves disciples, those who follow after Jesus and
call him master, if we refuse to let him transform every part of us.
None of us is perfect. All of us carry wounds. If we want to be his
disciples, we must let go of our pride and fear, our willful ignorance
and low expectations, and be vulnerable enough to let Jesus heal us.

Self-Pity

While some refuse help because they are in some way incapable of
admitting their wounds to themselves, others refuse help because
they actually *prefer* their wounds. Knowing full well that they are in
pain, and aware of the fact that someone is there to help them, they
choose misery over hope for a better life. Why would someone do
this, you ask? Because misery brings attention.

As children, we learned that crying gets us what we want. It got us
food when we were hungry, a kiss on the knee when we fell off our
bike, and the attention of mommy or daddy when fighting with our
siblings. (As the oldest sibling in my family, I am all too familiar with
the latter. All my sisters had to do was cry and call for my parents and
I was sure to be in trouble.) Although there was the risk of embar-
rassing ourselves in a tantrum, we knew that adults could hardly turn
away from a sad child, and, at the very least, would give us attention
if only to shut us up.

As adults, it may no longer be appropriate to fall on the ground
screaming for what we want, but some have realized that playing
on others' sympathy to get attention still works. People who are sad
and helpless get attention, even if it's only pity, from others. They
cling to their tragedies, losses, or ailments, knowing they will get
the affection they crave. They are open about their weaknesses to a

fault, share their sad stories to anyone who will listen, play up their physical limitations, and sulk in the corner. In their minds, sympathy is the same thing as love, and so they manipulate people into feeling sorry for them.

I am embarrassed to admit that a dark part of me can identify with this sort of thinking. Being ordinary gets you nothing, but being a sad case gets you sympathy. When I am not in a healthy place and begin to struggle with a task—maybe I shank a few golf balls off the tee or make some careless mistakes on the ball field—a part of me wants to sulk in my poor ability, pretend I have an injury, even play poorly *intentionally*, because then I might at least get some sympathy. It's the same feeling I can get on my birthday some years when nothing extraordinary is planned: a part of me almost *wishes* that people would forget about me, because then others would be compelled to show me sympathy later. We might have the opportunity to be healed of our wounds, to receive real happiness, but that would mean giving up the attention we know we'll get from them.

This distorted point of view doesn't give us what we really want. Pity gives us attention, yes, but it is not *quality* attention. Forcing someone to care about us is not the same as receiving selfless love. If we seek true love and genuine attention, sulking in the corner is not the way to go.

Not everyone who refuses to be healed does so out of a need for sympathy; in a far more destructive way, some people exploit their own wounds as a form of control over others. They have found that their greatest weakness yields the most effective power, and so they lean on it to get what they want. We see this in fairly benign situations: someone plays up a physical ailment to get a preferred seat or pretends not to understand something in order to have someone do it for them, but it can also be manipulative and destructive.

I have experienced this on more than a few occasions in which wounded people have used their points of pain to hold everyone else emotionally hostage, forcing others to walk around them on eggshells lest they become upset. It is the widow who attends the company Valentine's Day party only to mope, making others feel guilty about being in love; the curmudgeonly grandfather who refuses to go to the doctor but expects everyone to take care of him; the insecure friend who acts depressed whenever she sees her roommate having fun without her; the man in the wheelchair who becomes angry whenever anyone speaks of walking or running in his presence. Instead of doing what they can to overcome their weakness, they use it to control how others feel: Because they are sad, angry, lonely, in pain, disabled, or weak, everyone else must be as well.

On some level, we may have little incentive to let go of our wounds. Being healed means that we are just like everyone else, deserving no special treatment or attention; being healed means losing all the power. While they are by definition damaging, wounds offer an opportunity for some to feel important. Some would rather mope in their pain than do what is needed to heal.

For a disciple of Christ, this simply will not do.

Had the blind man preferred his ailment, seeing it as profitable to himself and a way to gain help from others, Jesus would certainly have let him remain that way; at no point in any of the Gospels does Jesus heal someone against his or her will or without faith. But had that man remained as he was, he would have never been able to follow Jesus as he did. God wants to set us free from all that burdens us—physical, emotional, moral, social—but God will not, and cannot, if we prefer to wallow in our own self-pity. If we wish to be Jesus's disciples, free of all burdens to follow him with our whole hearts, we must do as the blind man did, do as I did on that retreat how many years ago, and cry out to our Lord: "Son of David, have pity on me!"

Despair

For some, the issue is far worse than denying a wound or turning down help. What prevents them from allowing Jesus to heal them is not their own ignorance or a distorted vision of love that causes them to exploit their wounds. No, they are fully aware of what burdens them and would do anything to be whole again, but they do not believe it is possible. In their minds, the wound is too large, the burden too heavy. Nothing can be done to fix it. Left without hope, they believe they are inconsolable, irreparable, and unforgivable.

Grief over losing loved ones can lead to this kind of despair. A bone can be mended and a cut stitched, but when those we love have died, medicine can do nothing to bring them back. Once they are gone, they are gone forever. Never again will we feel the gentle touch of our loved ones, no longer will we hear their voices. Losing someone who meant a lot to us, who made us who we are and on whom we depended, can be devastating. To lose a spouse, a child, a caregiver—there is arguably no greater pain in all the world.

The same can be said about the devastation that comes from divorce, betrayal, or abandonment. I think of how I felt in college when my girlfriend of two years told me that she no longer wanted to be with me. The love that I thought existed between us, my belief that we would do anything for each other no matter the cost, disappeared in an instant. I was blindsided. That love, that person, that connection, was still alive and yet gone forever. How could a wound like that be healed? I think of how I felt when my closest confidant and strongest support for three years, a man who was both a business partner and beloved friend, decided that he no longer wanted to speak to me. Without so much as a warning and refusing to return my messages, he was gone. I was gashed. The friendship I had come to depend on, the mutuality that we shared in working out our salvation together, disappeared in an instant. Even though no death had occurred, in both cases, it felt as if a part of *me* had died. Something I loved had been lost forever. How could a wound like that—one of great betrayal—ever be truly healed?

With no hope of getting our loved ones back, it can be easy to feel inconsolable.

The same can be said of those who, because of an accident or illness, find themselves in a very different physical or mental state, unable to return to who they once were. What happens when our burdens are literal wounds with no cure? As a hospital chaplain, I once met a teenager who had suffered such great injuries from a car accident that the doctors had to remove one of his legs and suspected that he might have permanent nerve damage in his arms. This was a kid who lived to play soccer. Despite the advances in medicine, despite all that can be done with physical therapy and prosthetics, that boy would never fully recover from his wounds to be who he saw himself to be. There is no healing that could ever bring him back to who he had been before the accident.

For this reason, physical wounds are often accompanied by emotional ones. Whether it be a traumatic case of suddenly losing one's physical abilities, or merely the slow, inevitable loss that comes with growing old or chronic illness, it is impossible to overlook the fact that nothing can be done to return us to who we once were. This weighs heavy upon us. It can become easy to wonder what hope there is for healing.

The sense that something is *irreparable* about us overshadows our thoughts and begins to define who we are. Rather than simply being a person *with* a disease, disability, or condition, it becomes all too easy to identify ourselves by what we lack, to associate our very selves with the wounds we carry. And because our wounds are irreparable, it is only a matter of time before we see our*selves* as irreparable, beginning a downward spiral of feeling worthless and unlovable.

With that mindset, it's only a matter of time before we see ourselves as *unforgivable* as well. For if we no longer see ourselves as people *with* wounds but rather define ourselves *by* our wounds, how will we view ourselves when the wounds in question are moral ones? I've met many people who tell me they have done such terrible things that they are far beyond help. They can no longer see the goodness with which they were created, the love that holds them in being. When they look at themselves, all they can see is what they have done, and this disgusts them. They believe they are beyond saving.

We know from the Gospels that no one is beyond the healing touch of God. Jesus goes to those who are crippled, blind, possessed by demons, or even dead, and he restores them to life. He encounters prostitutes, tax collectors, shepherds, and foreigners—people as far from the Jewish covenant as one could find—and includes them in table worship. Jesus is so willing to invest in their lives that he touches even the most unclean people, those the religious elite consider ghastly, and calls them his friends. Nothing, it would seem, is too great for our Lord; no one, it seems clear, is too far gone.

Except for those who refuse to be healed. I think of Robert De Niro's character in the movie *The Mission*. So burdened with the guilt of murdering his brother, he refuses to eat and believes himself to be nothing more than garbage. When the priest offers him forgiveness, he does not accept it. Instead, he punishes himself by carrying his suit of armor—the instruments of his past misdeeds—everywhere he goes. Struggling up the waterfall and putting his life in danger, he refuses to let go of the suit of armor, despite the insistence of everyone else on the journey that it is unnecessary. Even though everyone else has moved on, even though a path is being offered to a better life, he cannot take it. He carries the weight himself, and it nearly kills him. How powerfully symbolic of the way despair gets in the way of God's mercy!

What's ironic about those who believe that they are unforgivable or too far removed from grace to be worthy of God is that they are a self-fulfilling prophecy. Scripture tells us that the only "unforgivable" sin is that against the Holy Spirit, something I interpret as the refusal of the grace of God: it is "unforgivable," not because it is so bad that God revokes his grace or seeks only to punish, but rather that only those willing to accept the grace of forgiveness can receive it. Someone remains unforgivable precisely because they do not want to be forgiven; they remain unforgivable because they deny the chance for God to be God.

While our physical lives on earth bear many instances of death, moments of apparent finality that leave us feeling inconsolable, irreparable, and unforgivable, we must always remember that death is not the end. Is that not the essence of our faith as Christians? We believe that in dying and rising, Jesus conquered death. In returning to his throne in heaven and inaugurating the inbreaking of his kingdom here on earth, we can be assured that what we experience on earth is but a veil of what exists, that every pain, burden, and weakness will one day be transformed into new life in a more final sense than we can imagine. Even when things seem lost here or without repair, we must never despair. We must never give up hope. Keep your eyes on the resurrection, and even death itself will fade away.

Christ: the Wounded Healer

In 1972, the great spiritual writer Henri Nouwen wrote a book called *The Wounded Healer*. In it, he suggests that the most successful healers are not those who present themselves as strong and perfect, but those who are honest about their own loneliness and pain. It's not difficult to see what he's getting at. Being in touch with one's own wounds can make a minister more approachable, easier to relate to, more empathetic. Having experienced what others have, the minister can enter relationships from a place of knowing, humbly walking alongside as a companion. Just as it is the one who has fallen into the pit who can show others the way out, so, too, is it the minister who has felt the sting of loss that can proclaim the joy of the resurrection most emphatically to those still in pain.

While Nouwen uses the term "wounded healer" exclusively in reference to pastoral ministers in a modern context, we can also see the essential archetype of a wounded healer: Jesus Christ. In the person of Jesus we see someone who was wounded in many ways. Despite being God, Jesus humbled himself to experience all that we do, except sin. His life wasn't sheltered and privileged. He allowed himself to be hurt along the way. He was betrayed, rejected, and abandoned by his own followers, felt sorrow at the death of his friend Lazarus, and experienced anguish in the Garden. At times he was weak and understood the humiliation of ridicule. This, of course, is not to forget the *physical* wounds that came as the result of being tortured and nailed to a cross, wounds that remained even after his resurrection.

This is a God who not only allowed himself to be wounded and die for a finite, sinful world, but maintained such wounds even in his glorified state. When he appears to Thomas in the upper room, his wounds have not been removed, filled in with a more perfect physical appearance. Not at all. There, seemingly for Thomas's sake, is a man with holes throughout his body to prove that he is the very one who suffered and died on the cross. But even more than that, there, for *everyone's* sake, is a man with holes throughout his body to prove that even our worst physical wounds can be redeemed. By appearing as he does, Jesus shows his disciples that one may be wounded and yet need not be defined by those wounds. He shows them how to acknowledge the memory of pain without letting it have control.

It's so subtle, yet quite elegant. For as much as our wounds—physical, emotional, moral, social—may be a burden to us here on earth, they are often a major catalyst in forming us into virtuous people. In our glorified states, we no longer want to be defined by them, but could we honestly remove them completely without removing a part of who we are? There is something distinct about my idiosyncrasies, scars, painful memories, and history of sin, and I'm not sure if I can be "me" without these things reminding me of where I've been and where I want to go. I am who I am, in part, because of the wounds that have shaped my life.

Following Jesus and allowing him to heal us does not mean that we will be magically made perfect. Not in heaven, and most certainly not here on earth. As we see in his own wounded body, there is a difference between being "glorified" and "aesthetically perfect." Even if we are his disciples, it is likely we will still bear the weight of certain pains; we will still have holes left unfulfilled. At least on earth, the dead will still be dead and what is lost will still be lost. Even the dry block of wood that was consumed by the fire left a trail of ashes. Like scars from long ago, some things will always hurt.

But they will no longer define us. When we follow Jesus and allow him to heal us, even the darkest, most painful parts of us are redeemed and made new, meaning that the way we approach these things will be completely different. No longer having a grip on us, our wounds will cease to hold us back, but will actually help us be greater heralds of the kingdom than ever before. Like Jesus evangelizing to Thomas, the marks of our own painful experiences will remain to show the glorious power of God.

If we want to be Jesus's disciples, if we want to follow after him with all our hearts, we must be vulnerable enough to acknowledge that we have wounds that need healing and willing enough to do what needs to be done to overcome them. But it's important to remember why we do this. The reason we need these things is not simply for our own sake. In allowing Jesus to redeem us and transform what is broken, our goal is not to be perfect or without discomfort. We seek Christ's healing to free us from the burdens that trap us, yes, but equally as important, we do so in order to announce to a broken world that no one needs to wallow in their pain alone. Healing is possible. That is, if we are willing to offer our wounds for God's glory.

What Must I Do?

1. Imagine yourself in my position, sitting in front of a bonfire with a block of wood in your hand. What would you write down as burdensome in your life? What do you want Jesus to take away. Spend some time in prayer naming these things and offering them up to God.

2. Have you ever refused help when you actually needed it? Why do you think you did this?

3. Sometimes we become so ashamed of a part of our life, so helpless in our inability to overcome a fault, that we hide it from others, ourselves, and even God. Is there a wound in your life that you have intentionally kept hidden? Maybe it's time to let it go, to let God heal you.

chapter six

Enemies

Then John said in reply, "Master, we saw someone casting
out demons in your name and we tried to prevent him
because he does not follow in our company." Jesus said to
him, "Do not prevent him, for whoever is not against you
is for you."

—Luke 9:49-50

When I was in college, I took a course called
"20th-Century Germany" in which we studied major
events like World War I, World War II, and so on.
Instead of using a traditional textbook, the course material consisted
entirely of primary sources, works like Erich Maria Remarque's *All
Quiet on the Western Front*, personal stories written by civilians during
World War II, and even Cold War propaganda from East Germany.
It was absolutely fascinating. While it was clear that horrific things
had happened in and because of the country—and I don't want to
diminish that—it was also clear how many people caught up in these
horrors were "normal" people, people no different from me. These
were not *evil* people. The vast majority of them were simply trapped
in the structures of social sin, unable to rise above the tremendous
forces dictating societal life. The course did not serve to exonerate an
entire nation, but it did help me to see how complicated the situation
was, how nearly impossible it would have been to act differently.
Villainizing an entire people was unfair to them and overlooked the
structures of sin in my own life.

At this same time I met a classmate who, in 2007—more than sixty years after the war had ended—vehemently refused to buy German cars and looked down on people who did. According to him, it was a disgrace to our forefathers who fought those evil people to support anything from that country.

This student had never been to Germany, likely never met a contemporary from that country, and had no direct connection to the war. Chances are, he did not even hear stories from a living relative who had fought in it. And yet, the anger and resentment of a previous generation still lived in him. Despite having no personal experience, and not being directly affected by the situation, a wedge remained between himself and part of the human family.

For a follower of Christ, resentment is a wedge that drives through the very mission we seek to carry out. It is a self-defeating attitude that we hold, undermining everything that we hope to build. The kingdom is not open simply to those who like us and are like us, but to all whom God has created and called back to Godself. Christ laid down his life not just for the good, but also for those who do evil. What separates the mission of Christ from the world is the insistence that we are to do more than simply tolerate our enemies. We are to love them. We are to lay down our lives for them. We are to give up the very idea that we have enemies.

If we want to be a true disciple of Christ, we must let go of the tribalism, grudges, and scapegoating that get in the way of loving all whom God loves.

Tribalism

It seems almost like a rite of passage that we must endure cliques in our teenage years: the jocks, nerds, preps, the whole lot. As burgeoning adults, we are at a time when we are finding ourselves, coming to know who we are and where we belong, and so we seek out clear markers of our identity. We associate with those who like the things we do, think the way we think, and look the way we look. In surrounding ourselves with such clearly (and narrowly) defined friends, we come to express who we are, and who we are not.

While this is certainly true, there is an irony to cliques: They help us form a general sense of identity, but they also stunt our growth and limit the extent to which we are able to grow as unique individuals. Cliques, by their very nature, are social groups that conform us to group-think, highlighting elements of the lowest common denominator of our personality in order to fit in. They reject differences as dangerous and exclude those who do not readily fit into simple categories, often in a hurtful way. We form an identity, yes, but not one that is particularly true to who we are.

As adults, we can all see how infantile and shallow this is, and yet, somehow we continue to fall prey to it. Even though we know we are at our best when surrounded by diverse ideas and people, we find ourselves continuing to seek out those who look, act, and think just like us. We surround ourselves with opinions that are comfortable, with people who affirm us, and readily scoff at those who potentially challenge our way of life. We like narrow categories and simple distinctions.

In extreme cases, this takes the form of open racism, nationalism, and xenophobia—horrendous acts of social evil still rabidly present in our world. Despite overwhelming scientific evidence to the contrary, many people still believe that a particular race or ethnicity is fundamentally superior to others, that certain groups of people are inherently smarter, kinder, better mannered, and "purer" than others; despite the overwhelming theological material to the contrary, there are still many who seek to humiliate, harm, divide, or even kill certain groups of people—in the name of God—because they believe that there is something inherently flawed in them.

This is disheartening, sickening, and completely incompatible with Christianity.

Of course, being prejudiced toward a certain people is not a binary question—either you are or you aren't—but rather something that exists on a spectrum and can be expressed in many subtle forms. We should be careful of *any* preconceived notions we hold, subtle barriers we place between ourselves and entire groups of people. This exists far beyond race and ethnicity, and is found, to some extent, in each and every one of us.

In our world today, the most noticeable form of this is when we attach qualifiers to our identity. In politics, it is the use of terms like "liberal" or "conservative" to express the totality of our identity; in the Catholic Church, it's words like "traditionalist," "progressive," and "Vatican II" preceding "Catholic"; we see this when the denominational affiliation—Catholic, Presbyterian, Baptist—becomes more important, even overshadows, the name of Christian. Just like our teenage selves, we continue to seek out markers of our identity, ways to define ourselves narrowly so as to conform to the identity of a group. We surround ourselves with those who like us and are like us, implicitly shutting out those who are different. *I'm not just a Catholic, I'm a traditional Catholic. That makes me distinct.*

It also undermines our mission in Christ.

For one, it oversimplifies the human experience. Just like the categories we used in high school to define ourselves and our peers, these categories say much less about us than we think: They are broad and shallow, offer little that is meaningful, and important nuances to our character get lost when we limit ourselves to a label. Look at any category of people and you will find not a uniform group but thousands of different opinions, personalities, hopes, and fears, held together by the broadest of similarities. The Republican party might have some key stances, but it is not a monolith; progressive Catholics may share an underlying principle, but they hardly agree on everything. My guess, actually, is that people in a given group are far more different than they are similar, bringing with them a unique set of experiences and a combination of traits that are neither liberal nor conservative but simply *them*. Identities cannot be simplified into two large boxes, diminished to a mere two-dimensional sliding scale. No, we are each a unique combination of self-contradiction that transcends easy categorization.

As a Franciscan, my experience is highly influenced by my life in fraternity. Over the past eight or so years, I have met hundreds of men who have professed vows within this Order, living in the way of St. Francis. We are, broadly speaking, all Franciscan, and there are certain markers that would distinguish us from other groups, say, the Dominicans, the police force, and NASA. But remove that overall category and you will find men who are so wildly different I wonder how we make it work. Despite our similar foundation, we share different visions of Church, skill sets, political leanings, preferences in prayer, and approach to the outside world. In many cases, our differences are not merely cosmetic, but present serious challenges for fraternal life. Are we all Franciscan? Absolutely. But that is hardly a sufficient enough qualifier to understand Br. Fred or Fr. John. The more we build our identity on such words, the more we diminish who we are and who we understand others to be.

Narrowly defining our religious identity divides the body of Christ. Every time I hear someone calling themselves a "trad" or saying they're not *that* type of Catholic, I hear St. Paul's words to the Corinthians ringing in my ears: "I'm with Apollos. I'm with Paul. I'm with Cephas. Is Christ divided?" (1 Corinthians 1:12). Defining our identity in this way involves cutting other identities off. In saying

I am this narrow qualifier, I am saying that I am *not* everything else. *Those things, those people, are not like me.* No matter how innocent it may seem, and even if we say it without any malicious intent, the act of categorizing ourselves and others into generic groups does damage to the human family because it adds false divisions and erects unnecessary walls, creating enemies.

Because, really, just as not everyone on "our side" is necessarily our friend or like us but a complex mix of varying thoughts and feelings, not everyone on the "other side" is necessarily against us or our enemy. It's funny how we forget that sometimes. I have no problem recognizing that the Franciscans are a large tent, that we are widely diverse in all things, but it is not so easy to remember that when I'm talking about the Dominicans, the police force, and NASA. Working from the limited knowledge I have of those groups, my brain naturally applies what I know about the category to every member of that group, assuming, rather foolishly, that they are all the same. If I have a favorable opinion about the group, I will be inclined to treat new acquaintances favorably, but if my opinion is negative, there is a part of me that will assume, even if just subconsciously, something negative about a new acquaintance.

I believe we put far more limits on Christ than he puts on us. We prefer a smaller, more unified Church when Christ goes to the outer limits of society to include the least likely candidates. When I read the Gospels and see how Jesus interacts with those around him, what I see is the exact opposite of tribalism, the exact opposite of circling the wagons, the exact opposite of surrounding oneself with the pure and holy. The world divides, but Christ brings together.

Stop dividing Christ. Stop making enemies where they don't exist. Stop relying on narrow markers of identity so we can feel at home in ourselves by excluding others. There is room in the kingdom of God for us all. Our role as followers of Christ is not to divide the world into categories, but to bring together the many disparate and distant peoples as one. Never forget: "There is neither Jew nor Greek, there is neither slave nor free person, there is not male and female; for you are all one in Christ Jesus" (Galatians 3:28).

Grudges

Of course, enemies do not simply come about from groups that are different from us. Sometimes, the objects of our strongest resentment are those who are quite similar to us, those former friends and loved ones who betrayed our trust and hurt us deeply. When expectations are dashed and something we loved goes missing, it can be very easy to respond with hate, harboring unrelenting feelings of ill-will toward others.

In my life, resentment has often surfaced as a defense mechanism against grief. After being broken up with or betrayed by a friend, my immediate reaction was that of immense sadness, but these emotions are difficult to integrate. Rather than dealing with our sadness directly, being vulnerable with how we feel and accepting the reality of our loss, it is much easier to convert our sadness into anger, replacing our unreturned love with hatred. *I never loved her anyway! He was such a jerk, I hope he gets what's coming to him!* How sad it is to see people unable (or unwilling) to deal with the pain of sadness, protecting themselves from their true feelings with the burning anger of resentment!

I think back to those times when I was so distraught about losing someone I loved that I began looking for things to hate about them. To protect myself from the sadness of happy memories, I began to read my pain and anger back into our time together, remembering and retelling those stories in a new way. It was easier to accept that this person was horrible to me all along—they had *always* been manipulative, domineering, and rude—than to accept that I had lost something truly special. We are often more comfortable telling ourselves a lie and creating an enemy than dealing with the painful truth of loss.

This is a common defense mechanism when dealing with any form of loss. I once knew a guy who loved his job for many years. It was a difficult job at times, and he by no means was free of frustration, but he generally liked what he did. But when his position was eliminated and he was effectively fired, you should have heard the way he spoke about his boss and that company even years later! I'll never know for sure what was true or not, whether he actually had reason to be angry, but he held onto resentment toward that company *long* after he found a new job, and that resentment absolutely controlled him.

And so we hold onto grudges. We harbor hatred. We cut people out of our lives. It is a way to cope with the feelings we have, to get back at those who have hurt us. They will get nothing but a cold shoulder from us, nothing but unmitigated disrespect. That will teach them. That will show them how much they hurt us and how little we think of them. Right?

Sadly, no.

The unfortunate irony about most grudges and feelings of resentment is that they are only ever known by us: the people we hold grudges against are hardly ever aware of what is going on inside us. My ex-girlfriend never knew the things I said about her; the friend that betrayed me doesn't know how my heart burns with anger at the thought of him; my friend's boss probably never gave another thought to her one-time employee. No, resentment does not hurt the other, nor does it bring us solace. It fills us with anger that can only eat us up inside.

I remember having a problem with someone in my novitiate class. He did so many things that annoyed me, and I found myself frustrated even by his very presence. To show my dislike of him, I gave him the silent treatment, acting passive-aggressively toward him—things to really show that I did not like him. I told my spiritual director about this one day, and I'll never forget his response: "How's that working out for you?" There was a smugness to his voice, the sort of voice you use with a smile when you already know the answer. As I thought about it, I realized that it wasn't working at all: this other novice had no idea that we were even in a feud! Here I was fuming with anger, losing sleep at night, and he hadn't thought of me even once.

While some grudges are between people with routine contact and so public showings of disapproval are common, the vast majority of resentment occurs when the other party isn't even around. Friends and family members, holding onto a feud from how many years ago, choose not to talk with one another. *That will teach them!* The sad reality is that resentment does not teach anyone anything because it is something that only exists in our hearts. No one will ever know the extent of it but us, and so it cannot hurt anyone *but* us. No one is hurt by it quite like us, and yet no one prevents us from letting it go. Resentment, as the widely attributed quote goes, is "like drinking poison and expecting the other person to die." It will never succeed in giving us what we want.

I'm not sure we can complete the journey with Christ if we carry with us so much baggage. When our heart is filled with anger, there is less room for love; when we have a list of people with whom we refuse to associate, our ability to preach the kingdom of God becomes inhibited. What if the very thing that Jesus asks us to do is to welcome the one who cast us away? What if we find that the people who have hurt us actually precede us in the kingdom, and the only thing that's required for us to enter is that we seek reconciliation?

The way of Christ is one of mercy and forgiveness. This does not mean forgetting we've been hurt or naively pretending it didn't happen; it is simply showing an openness to a future relationship. True reconciliation takes time and is not possible without the willingness of both parties, but if we refuse to let go of the past, holding onto our past pains and slights, no progress will ever be made. Unless we are able to let go of the resentments that hold us back, remembering that we, too, are the recipients of undeserved mercy and forgiveness, we will never be able to love in the way Jesus does.

Scapegoats

The idea of a scapegoat is an extremely old religious and cultural practice. All the sins and ills of a community are ritually transferred to an animal, generally a goat, and it is either driven out of the city or sacrificed, symbolically eliminating the problems of the entire group. Much like my retreat experience with the block of wood in the previous chapter, it is a simple and cathartic way to deal with one's problems.

That is, unless you're the goat...or you actually want to fix your problems.

For me, what was so powerful about burning the block of wood was not the burning itself or tricking myself into thinking these things would actually go away now. Rather, it forced me to accept that there were things I needed to change in my life. As I said, it was the writing, not the burning, that brought about change in my life. The problem with scapegoats, often, is that they are a quick fix, something that does not require real change but serves as nothing more than the recipient of our disgust. We can project our anger, but the anger is never addressed. When the object of our anger is a block of wood, no harm is done, except to ourselves. When it is a goat—or worse yet, individuals or entire groups of people—this practice can be harmful to everyone involved.

While most of us don't go through such rituals these days, I think many of us maintain scapegoats. The biggest reason we continue to have enemies in our lives is because we *need* enemies. Why? Because enemies make us feel superior. *At least I'm not like them!* They fill us with passion and give us a sense of confidence and direction. When there is evil to be rooted out, we rise to the occasion. I notice this all the time on the internet. Trolls will bash the Catholic Church, presenting themselves as the purest of Christians, criticizing what they believe to be wrong with us. Often, I will engage, presenting proof to show them that what they say is untrue, but they refuse to hear it. They call me a liar and deceiver, reverting to their original character attacks as proof that I cannot be trusted. "Wouldn't it be wonderful," I ask them, "if you were wrong about these things and Catholics *weren't* actually pagan heretics? Shouldn't you be *glad* to hear that we are actually on the same team?" They're not—they want an enemy, a source of corruption to show how pure they are.

When we can identify someone else as evil and wrong, we once again create confirmation that we are holy and right. A dark part of us looks for people doing horrible things so we can feel better about the path we have chosen.

In 2016, the world saw a tremendous growth in misinformation aimed at deceiving voters. Thousands of fake websites were created slandering different candidates, companies, and celebrities, and articles with the slightest semblance of reputability were circulated on the internet. Those who were not emotionally involved in the subject or were able to step back and think critically about what they were seeing found themselves confused at how anyone would believe it. *How did this stuff spread so fast? It's obviously made up to get people angry.* This question, I think, is best answered with another question: Why wasn't there an onslaught of fake *good* news? People were willing to share things that were outrageous, hurtful, and slanderous about their opponent, and had no problem believing and sharing it, because it made them more comfortable with the stance they had already taken. People so hungered for validation that they were quick to accept the easiest answer that offered it. Critical reflection need not apply.

At the root of this is a far more fundamental issue, something that existed long before the 2016 election cycle: For thousands of years, in every culture and religion, there has been an unsatisfied need to give an explanation for the existence of evil. *Why do bad things happen?*

The easiest answer, the one that can explain away all of our ills without challenging the notion of God or placing any responsibility on us, is to look for an enemy that caused it. I dare say, this is why some Christians *love* the devil. I do not mean they are worshipers of Satan, but that they are infatuated by the idea of a devil, a being that they can blame for all the ills of the world. Blaming the devil offers a source to explain away all of our problems, an object for all of our hatred.

Am I suggesting that the devil doesn't exist or that said demon is not capable of producing evil? Of course not. But one has to question the motive of someone who speaks of the devil with such frequency and blames him for *everything*. This form of scapegoating takes all responsibility off of humanity, oversimplifies the question of evil, and hides from difficult questions of theology like, "How can there be an all-powerful God and still be evil?" If there is also an all-powerful evil being responsible for it, then we can place all our anger in one place and move on, but it will not give us the satisfaction that we really need. It is a cheap answer to an important question, and it conditions us to blame others for our own problems.

For many years I held a lot of resentment toward my high school baseball coach. Two years in a row I was told I was the best shortstop on the team, but that because of the team's needs elsewhere, I would have to play a position I was not as good at. There was no doubt in my mind that in doing so, he cost me a chance to play college baseball. For years, as I sat frustrated with the lost opportunity, the crushed dream. I blamed him. Had he played me at shortstop, given me the opportunity to do what I did well, I might have even gotten a scholarship. My life would have been different.

I brooded, and I resented. I treated him as a scapegoat. Rather than focus on the other factors involved, taking ownership of my own life, recognizing that I could have worked harder, played better, sought out other opportunities, *accepted that maybe there were simply players who were far better than me,* it was much easier to blame everything on him, to hold a grudge, to bottle up the anger for years.

So it is with all scapegoats. Rather than accept that an issue is complex without an easy solution, it is far easier to blame it on an entire ethnic group; rather than take responsibility for the mistakes we've made, it's far safer to blame a subordinate. Whether it be our failed relationships, unsuccessful careers, health problems, financial insecurities, or simply a lack of happiness, the temptation is to look for someone or something to blame so that we can defer responsibility and avoid the hard work to eliminate the problem.

We want an enemy, a sacrifice, a target for our anger. *Just tie up everything that's wrong on another helpless being, and let it go!* It may be cathartic. It may even make the problem go away for a bit. But it cannot last. While we might feel immediate gratification, pinning our problems on an enemy will always leave us worse off in the long run. Our anger—not the problem itself—will be our downfall. In our anger, we sacrifice the innocent lamb.

I truly believe you cannot hate and be a follower of Christ. If you hate those who hate him, you unwittingly become what you hate: an outsider who brings evil into the world. In choosing a scapegoat, projecting our anger onto another, we disregard Christ's command to love our enemies and make of ourselves an enemy of Christ.

We Are One Body

At the root of all our fear, anger, hatred, and division is a lie: There is not enough love and goodness to go around. We live with the notion that goodness is in strict supply, that there is a scarcity of happiness to go around. Like children, we feel like we must compete for mommy's love. *I cannot be happy at the same time as another. If he gets something, that means that I won't get it; there won't be enough for me.* Approaching the world with a "survival of the fittest" mentality, we can't help but see our neighbor's success as our defeat.

Could there be a more foolish mindset in all the world?

There are more than enough resources to feed, clothe, and comfort every human being on earth if only we would share. We also know that there is more to life than eating and drinking. The things that truly matter—love, sacrifice, justice, mercy—are renewable resources with no end. Unlike material goods that can only be consumed by one person and then are lost, the gifts that truly matter only grow the more they are shared. There is no need to worry about having enough.

More importantly, the idea that our neighbor's success is anything other than our own success is utterly contrary to the kingdom. Despite the way the world often works, we know as Christians that we are not divided or separate, but of one family. Each and every one of us was created by the same God, infused by the same Spirit. Our DNA might be different, but the source of our life, the image imprinted on our souls, and the purpose for walking this earth is all the same: We were created by God to be adopted sons and daughters, loving and serving our God in the kingdom. It may be hard to see sometimes, given our difference in opinions, nationalities, languages, and backgrounds, but the fact is we are all on the same team, created as one human race.

Among those who are Christians, our bond is even deeper, as we have shared in the one redemptive bath for all ages. Across denominational lines, we accept the unique bond we share in Christ, that we are of one body, redeemed and sanctified in his blood. As St. Paul writes to the Corinthians, "If one part suffers, all the parts suffer with it; if one part is honored, all the parts share its joy" (1 Corinthians 12:26). There is no scarcity in Christ, no competition in his body. Such an idea is self-defeating. It is, as the cliché goes, stealing from Peter to pay Paul. We all share in the same central banking!

Whenever I find myself jealous of another's success and so gravitate toward a narrow view of the world, hold on to past slights, or project my problems onto another, I find it helpful to take a step back so that I can get a wider view. The only reason I'm willing to exclude or hurt others is because I have convinced myself that they do not go with me. But how can that be true? We are one body. We are one family. When good things happen to my family, when a teammate of mine receives glory, I rejoice with them. So it should be with all I encounter.

What Must I Do?

1. It can be hard to admit to ourselves that we have any prejudices against others, but hiding from them doesn't make them go away. Do you find that you struggle to get along with a certain type of person? Where might that feeling come from, and how do you overcome it?

2. Are there people in your life that you refuse to be around or forgive for past sins? Do you ever find yourself thinking about ways that you have been hurt, long after the situation has occurred?

3. Since the time of St. Paul, Christians have used the image of "the body of Christ" to describe the Church. Take some time to meditate on this image. How does it affect your approach to certain "enemies" when you see them as intimately connected to yourself?

chapter seven

Power

Though he was in the form of God, Jesus did not regard
equality with God something to be grasped. Rather, he
emptied himself, taking the form of a slave, coming in human
likeness; and found human in appearance, he humbled
himself, becoming obedient to death, even death on a cross.

—PHILIPPIANS 2:6-8

A professor of mine once offered the opinion that the
Church of Christ sold out in the fourth century when
it wed itself to Rome and became the official religion
of the Empire. Being that he was a Protestant, and as I was growing
in my (tribal) identity as a Catholic at the time, it was easy for me to
become defensive and dismiss his words as those of an anti-Catholic
"Protester." *What does he know? He's just trying to criticize the Catholic
Church.*

Years later, I can now see that he was making a very legitimate
point.

Prior to the year 313, Christians in most areas of the Roman
Empire were an extreme minority and had almost no influence
whatsoever. Persecution was not universal, and largely dependent on
the region and who was in charge, but Christians enjoyed no legal
protections and were subject to harsh punishments with no means
of defense. Truly, they were outsiders. After 313, when Emperor
Constantine allowed Christianity to be practiced freely—and then

made it the official religion of Rome just a decade later—all of this changed. Christians now found themselves in positions of authority and influence, leading the government, military, and church at once. They were not only afforded new rights and protections, they were the ones enforcing them. Just like that, Christians, once insignificant outsiders, wielded tremendous power over others.

This, no doubt, presented them with a profound opportunity to transform the Empire to more resemble the kingdom of God—an opportunity that many would jump at—but it also presented a major shift in identity from what Jesus expected of his disciples. His witness was not of power and authority, but of meekness and humility. His beatitudes reveal a desire for a Church that knows nothing of strength but everything of weakness, a people that identifies with the poor, oppressed, and outcast. How does one reconcile the requirements of discipleship that Jesus outlined with the requirements of running an empire such as Rome? No matter how virtuously people approach their offices, it is difficult to profess humility, to identify with the poor, and to take up one's cross when one is of the ruling class, controlling armies and sentencing others to the cross. One necessarily has an effect on the other.

While I do not completely agree with my professor that the Church of Jesus Christ sold out at this moment and somehow ceased to be the authentic sacrament of salvation on earth, I do agree with his underlying principle: Wielding power and influence undermines the very foundation of the Gospel. Throughout our history, there has been a rather strange belief that Christianity is better off the more we can control the world—political, economic, and social power can be wielded for the good, and so we should seek it wherever possible. *Imagine all we could do with that power,* we think. *If only we had the structures, if only we had more money to do the work of God, if only we could make laws enforcing God's kingdom.* We have come to believe that power and influence are not only helpful to the task of evangelization, but a constitutive element of it. (This, of course, despite the exponential growth of the Church without any of these things in its first three centuries.)

I believe the case for Christ is not only weaker when we possess greater wealth and authority, but we undermine his entire mission when we are at all concerned with gaining more of it. If we want to follow after him, we must let go of the influence of our status, the agency of our own independence, and the kingdoms that we build for ourselves. The path to Christ is not one that can be won through might; it must be redeemed through weakness.

Status

A few years ago, on one of my missions outside of the United States, I was scandalized by the actions of another friar. We were driving in his native country when he was pulled over for clearly violating a not-so-minor traffic law. Pulled over on the side of the road with the police officer behind us, the friar decided to go on the offensive. Rather than just sitting in the car and waiting for the officer to approach us, acknowledging that he had done something wrong and accepting the consequences for it, he jumped out of the car and jovially called to the police officer, "Hello officer! Don't worry, I'm a *priest*! There's no problem here, I'm a *Franciscan*!"

I was so humiliated, so shocked, so filled with anger, that I nearly vomited.

Forgetting for a second that this man had just committed a serious moving violation and potentially put his foreign guests in danger—you know, *that* small thing!—here was a man, professed in the way of life of St. Francis of Assisi and calling himself a "lesser brother," a man who had been ordained a priest of Jesus Christ to imitate his humble service, using his status as a "respected" man of society to get himself out of trouble. He believed that who he was in the Church made him above the law and so invoked the names of St. Francis and Jesus as a means of power over the police officer. *Surely, you can't give a ticket to a Franciscan priest! Don't you know who I am?*

Without any exaggeration, I honestly do not know if I have ever been more angry and disgusted in my entire life. Something struck a nerve in me, and, I kid you not, I did not speak for almost twenty-four hours. Here was a man invoking the names of two humble men—men known for renouncing power and going to extraordinary lengths to engender humility in themselves—in order to gain for himself the exact opposite of what they stood for. To hear him flaunt those names with such arrogance, flashing them about like they were prized currency, holding his status over another to get what he wanted, to think about how much damage this man had done in his life to the image of the Church and Order, living with such entitlement as a representative of both. It was like my brain shorted out from the dissonance and could only display the message "does not compute." I did not want to call him my brother. *What do you know about St. Francis? What do you know about the humility of Christ, the man who accepted even death on a cross for sins that he didn't even commit to show his love for the lost and forgotten?*

I have never been more disappointed in a friar in my life than this.

Unfortunately, such abuses of power are not uncommon. Since this experience, I have found myself acutely aware of its existence throughout the Church and viscerally allergic to any situation in which Christians use their status for personal gain. It's the bishop who wears extraordinarily expensive garments and expects to be treated like a prince, who wants his priests and seminarians to wash *his* feet; the deacon who knows more about being served at luxurious galas than serving the homeless; the religious who wears his or her habit in public so a generous parishioner will pay the restaurant bill; even the parish councilor who believes his or her status at the parish earns them special treatment from the rest of the parishioners. We can look to almost every facet of the Church and find those who use and abuse their power for personal gain, and we can admonish them for it. Clearly, this is not what Jesus wanted for his disciples.

And yet, in doing so, we might fall prey to our own hypocrisy.

As I've seen such horrible acts in our Church and reflected on my experience with this other friar, I've become more and more aware of how guilty *I* am, albeit in less obvious ways, of committing the same sins. These acts of arrogance might be public and extreme, but as I think of them more, I find them to be a rather helpful mirror into my own life. Like the Pharisee who looked at the tax collector and said, "Thank God I am not like him," I undermine the very Gospel I seek to defend when I see only others' faults and not my own. I may not *flaunt* my power over others, but I know that I can get quite defensive when someone disrespects or challenges me, especially on issues I've studied for years; as much as I say I am a follower of Christ in the way of St. Francis, I know I hardly respond to rudeness the way they would. In these situations, I do not always resemble the calm and unaffected Jesus standing before Pilate. No, my blood begins to boil, my defenses go up, and I'm ready with a snide retort. *Who do you think you are telling me that I'm wrong? Don't you know that I'm a priest, that I have a graduate school degree in this? How dare you speak to me that way!*

Not exactly the humility of the follower of Christ.

Within our workplaces, communities, leisure life, and even families, there are titles upon titles upon titles, all encouraging us to assert our place and importance over others. Just as the religious world can use words like "father" and "cardinal" to command authority, so too can "executive" and "doctor" be wielded as weapons. We can be VIPs or be considered platinum members in our purchases, earning us special treatment. Even in our families: One does not need to be royalty to understand the power that family titles like "uncle" or "grandma" can have. While at face value titles serve as nothing more than a designation of relationship or responsibility, the fact is we act differently around someone because of their title. We give greater (or lesser) respect because of it. And when that happens—when titles wield power in accepted ways—preferential treatment becomes the expectation of those who hold them. One's status becomes a form of power over others.

Of course, one does not always need a title to have status. In today's world, we are becoming more aware of how class, gender, and race have subconsciously and unintentionally provided privileges to certain people for years. Straight, white, middle-class men (like myself) have enjoyed treatment in society unknown to others, and have grown accustomed to it. It is subconsciously *expected* that when we turn on the TV we will find someone who looks and sounds like us. I know this because when there is a sports panel of all black men, when the news consists of two female anchors, when someone speaks with an accent or broken English, I've seen people get annoyed. *This is racist! How sexist!* They recognize that, for the first time, something does not speak directly to their experience and they feel excluded. When, for many years, every single person on television looked and sounded like them—when entire other peoples were being excluded—nothing seemed awry. To them, there was nothing racist or sexist about a panel of four white men on television, nothing exclusive or unfair about it. It was accepted as normal, and so it became expected.

When something expected is taken away, tempers flare.

In the United States, this is precisely the case for Christians who have struggled to live in a world moving toward religious pluralism. Turn back the clock and you will see a nation—even a Western World—that was largely dominated by "Christian values." Even in places where there is an official separation between Church and State, Christians, being the majority, have always dictated the laws and norms of society. Christmas trees were commonplace in civil places, the Ten Commandments appeared on courthouse steps, the word "God" on money and in pledges. To be Christian was to be the dominant status, often blind to how others did not enjoy such cultural privileges. As the world becomes more aware of this blind-spot and attempts to make things more fair—incorporating other religious symbols into the mix and removing Christian ones so as to remain objective—some Christians feel slighted. *We're being persecuted for being Christian!* The loss of exclusive status, *the loss of power*, is a tough pill to swallow for some.

But it must be taken.

As Christians, we are followers of a man who renounced a heavenly status that owed him the greatest power and authority in all of Creation. He did not claim his kingship or remind people of who he was. When persecuted, Jesus didn't puff up his chest and demand respect. Rather, he did all that he could to strip himself of anything that would serve as a means of power. He was financially poor and a cultural outcast. He took no title and even rebuked his followers for using them. Even symbolically, he washed the feet of his disciples—the job reserved for the lowest of slaves—to ensure that his status would always be remembered as that of a servant. In every way that he could, Jesus stripped himself of anything that owed him privilege or power. In the eyes of the world, he was but an insignificant laborer from a backwater town.

CASE COLE, OFM | *Let Go*

If we want to follow after him and go where he goes, we must
renounce any power and privilege that comes with our status so to
be humble servants as he was. As much as our position in society
may make others think we are important, as much as our titles may
make others treat us differently, it is important to remember that we
are all helpless children in the eyes of God. Our status in the world
(or even the Church) means nothing in the eyes of God. It does not
make us better or worse than others, and it most certainly doesn't
mean we are owed any special treatment. In fact, it might actually
demand more humility from us because we have a farther way down
than others.

Independence

I imagine that when most people think about the difficulties of
joining religious life, the first thing that comes to mind is the vow
of chastity. How could it not? In our sex-crazed world, the idea of
willingly living a chaste life seems absurd, if not impossible. It was
the aspect of this life that I was most worried about when I entered,
and it remains a major challenge for each and every friar as we live
this life.

But it's not the most difficult aspect of religious life. Especially not
at first.

Of the three vows (and all the other commitments we make as
religious) obedience is by far the most difficult. In fact, I would
venture to guess that if people of our day were to really think about
it themselves, they would find it to be even *more* bizarre than a life
of chastity. *Wait, you have to do what someone else tells you to do?* We
live in a world where people do what they want, when they want,
how they want. We define freedom not in the classical sense of "the
ability to do what is good," but simply "the ability to do *anything* we
desire regardless of its benefit or utility." To take a vow of obedience,

agreeing to do what one's superior says simply because the superior says it, is the antithesis of a good life for so many. Obedience as a vow includes more than just direct orders from a superior, but a committed relationship of accountability, transparency, support, and humility to an entire household of other religious; taking the vow means loving and serving people that you don't necessarily love or even like, people that you did not choose, who annoy you as much as they please you. Looking at it through that lens, it seems positively *ludicrous. Why would anyone choose that?*

Honestly? Because I think it's the key to the kingdom of God.

We have an infatuation with independence in our world. Especially in the United States, an ethos of absolute autonomy runs through our blood, a fear of any strong central authority that may tell us what to do or how to live our lives. *I'm fine on my own, thank you very much. I don't need the government or community telling me what I can or cannot do on my own property.* We value those who are self-sufficient and look down on those who ask for help. Look at the American Dream itself: someone who begins with nothing, receives no help from anyone, but "pulls themselves up by their own bootstraps" to become rich and successful. Could there be a more telling myth of what we value in this country? Of all our values, autonomy might be our most primary.

Compare this to the values of the kingdom of God. Where do you think independence and absolute autonomy rank among Jesus's teachings? I would venture to guess they don't even exist. The idea of being autonomous in God's kingdom is a contradiction in terms! Is not the purpose of the kingdom to be in union with God? Is not the purpose of following Jesus to acknowledge that *he* is king, not us, so that we may love and serve him in whatever he asks of us? The idea of following Jesus, and yet doing what we want, reserving for ourselves some level of freedom that God cannot touch, simply doesn't make sense. A disciple is not someone who likes Jesus and goes along with *most* of what he says. No, a disciple is someone who turns his or her *entire* will over to God and trusts that God will lead them along the right path.

Religious life, at its best, attempts to model this. And it can be awful.

The first two years of being a friar were extremely difficult when it came to obedience. Our directors determined every aspect of our lives. We were given schedules that told us when we prayed, when we worked, when we ate, and even when we were to have fun (yes, forced fun is a real thing in religious life). We were often given what I believed to be asinine tasks to complete and forced to renounce almost all of our independence. Of particular difficulty for many of us was the insistence that we ask permission to do things that were otherwise commonplace in our lives before, things like making a phone call, using the internet, leaving the property, and even spending money.

I remember having a "discussion" with one of the leaders once, frustrated with how infantilizing the experience was and trying to understand the benefit of being treated this way. *Why do we need to be treated like children?* I'm not sure if the answer I received quite justifies the level of childishness we had to endure at times, but I completely agree with the value they were trying to instill: There is something to be gained in having to ask for permission. In other words, in a world that tells us to do what we want, when we want, how we want, it is important to remember that we are not the rulers of our own kingdom. Having to acknowledge that we are responsible to someone else, accountable to another with the distinct possibility that we may not get what we want, reminds us that we are not islands separate from everyone else. What we do affects others, and what we do is not solely for our own benefit. As Christians, we are but servants in everything we do.

Following Jesus means trading the independence of our will for the obedience to his.

But really, it's even more than that. As important as our wills are, and as difficult as it might be to give up the autonomy of our own decisions, I think there is a form of independence that is even more difficult to relinquish: our personal agency. We want to do things for ourselves without having to ask for help.

Coincidentally enough, the most incapacitating experience of my life took place during the same year of my formation. (It was truly a foundational year of humility for me!) After many years of playing baseball and lifting weights, my shoulder finally gave out, and I was forced to have major surgery on my dominant arm. Just like that, at twenty-five years old, it was like I was a child again, completely dependent on others to help me with basic tasks. At meals, I had to sit at the table while someone prepared my food, cut it up, and then cleared my place. For the first few days, I had to have a classmate come into my room and help me get changed in the morning. Talk about *infantilizing*.

While I was capable enough to handle all of my personal needs in the bathroom (thank God!), it was a humbling experience that reminded me how truly fragile our lives are. Especially when we are young, we live with a sense of invincibility. Not only do we subconsciously believe that nothing will ever happen to us, but we take for granted the abilities we have to take care of ourselves. When our body and mind are functioning, when we're able to do things without anyone's help, we rarely appreciate the importance of depending on others.

Not after surgery. Not when we're sick. Not in old age.

Just as I would never wish the asinine structures of my novitiate on anyone else, forcing them to ask permission to do just about everything, I would never wish major surgery or sickness on anyone. But there is definitely a part of me that wishes, hopes beyond hope, that every Christian will be forced into experiences that necessitate humility and dependence upon others. As uncomfortable and debilitating as it is, there is something so incredibly important for disciples of Christ in being stripped of one's independence, of being left bare and broken without any possibility of getting yourself out of trouble.

We rely too much on our own agency, and this is a problem. Whether it be our decision-making or physical capabilities, our wealth and security, our intelligence or wit, there is an innate sense in all of us that we can and must take care of ourselves. *My life is my responsibility. I can't assume that anyone is going to help me.* As a result, we often don't even know how to ask for help when we need it. Some even feel dejected and worthless when they do, believing their life to be a failure because they were not able to take care of themselves. Autonomy is such a value for some that they would rather suffer alone than give up their independence to rely on another.

While that might be valued in a capitalist world, it is completely antithetical to the kingdom of God. We are not independent, but made one in the body of Christ. We do not rely on our own power, but recognize that we are all weak without Christ. There is but one source of strength in our world, one source of freedom, and that is God.

If we want to follow Jesus, we have to let go of the notion that we are in any way on our own or determine our own fate. Our decisions are not our own. Our abilities are not our own. Our lives are not our own. Those who remain independent, relying on their own strength separate from Jesus, will all one day realize that their strength is not enough. Be obedient to Jesus, and you will be truly free. Rely on him for help, and you will be truly strong.

Kingdoms

Few of us will ever be rulers of sovereign nations. In fact, just going on the statistics, it's a pretty safe bet to say that no one reading this book will ever become a king or queen, president or prime minister. (Although a shout out to the pope if he gets his hands on this!) The number of people who are given this much power and authority— absolute in most cases—is astronomically small. The idea of closing this book by telling Christians that they need to "let go" of their kingdoms in order to be true disciples would seem to be, at best, an oddly specific requirement applying to only a few dozen people in the world.

So it may seem. But one does not need a sovereign nation to have a kingdom.

In my experience, kingdoms are all around us. They exist on a geo-political level, yes, but they also exist anywhere someone wields power they want to retain. Throughout all the many subcultures of our lives there exist norms and mores, social hierarchies and distinctive roles, people with power and people without it, all operating distinct from the common authority of the larger culture. Existing within a bubble, a small enclave of social interactions removed from others, they can take on the same authoritarian structures as nations, and despite the minuscule level of actual authority or responsibility, can drive people mad as they seek to be in control.

The easiest and most common of these kingdoms to grasp is the family structure. Within each home are certain expectations, social dynamics, rules, hierarchies, and even cultures. *How my family operates is different from other families.* This is always a strange thing to become aware of as we get older. Having lived in our little bubbles for however many years, we spend the night at a friend's house only to find that they pray a blessing over the food differently than we do; that they have inside jokes that mean nothing to us; that their dad sits at a different spot at the table and the mom has different rules for table manners. Most unsettling of all to young kids is realizing that what they believed to be completely normal, because that's the only way they have ever known it, is actually quite peculiar. *You don't refer to the cabinets in the garage by name?* (You can blame my younger sister for starting that trend…) In a tiny and bizarre way, each family lives as its own little kingdom, complete with its own set of rules… and rulers.

In the most extreme cases, these rulers take the form of Don Corleone, the patriarchal leader of an organized crime dynasty, ruling very much like a crazed king over his kingdom, using violence and civil authority to keep the kingdom alive and powerful. While this is hardly relatable to most, take a step back, imagine a family patriarch or matriarch who cannot be questioned and expects obedience even from siblings, and it becomes all too common. It's one thing to be the oldest and wisest in the family, taking on the responsibility of leading the family as one is fit. It is a completely different situation, however, to be in such a position against the will of the rest of the family, demanding subservience without humility. I'm thinking of the grandmother who expects preferential treatment from her children but refuses to ever apologize when she makes a mistake; the man who believes he has absolute authority over the lives of his wife and kids and balks at any questioning; the siblings who compete for influence after their parents have passed, seeking to get the other family members to look to them for direction. Even within the most loving and non-mobster families, some members may rule as if their family were a kingdom, focused more on control than on relationships. This is a kingdom worth divesting.

So, too, are the kingdoms of workplaces. Just as in the case of families, there are the extreme examples of CEOs and the super rich all jockeying for power over a particular market, willing to kill to obtain even more power, but there are far more common occurrences in our ordinary offices. *Here is where territories are truly marked and battles really fought.* I'm talking about the menial, bureaucratic jobs where one person is in charge of some insignificant task but refuses to let anyone take an inch of their authority. I'm talking about the person who has done something one way for decades and throws a tantrum if anyone dares mess with his or her system. I've seen it at the DMV, and I've seen it at major universities. There might be a more efficient way to do something, even a more competent person in the office to take care of it, but it doesn't matter. The person in charge of that task is in charge, and no one is going to question their authority. *This is my kingdom.*

What I find so interesting about these situations is the amount of emotional energy that is often attached to such unimportant tasks. In novitiate, when arguments would start over planning the daily liturgies or organizing the kitchen, we would often paraphrase Sayre's Law: "The tempers were so high because the stakes were so low." Truly, the less important something is, the more some will fight to maintain control of it. People in these situations tend not to care as much about the task itself or the well-being of those related to it as they do about the mere fact that they have control over something. Tempers flare, not because the task is inherently important to anyone's life, but because someone's authority is being questioned, a kingdom is being challenged. Originally meant to describe academia, the law is true for any kingdom: local government offices, religious novitiates, PTO meetings, faculty subcommittees, and yes, even the Church proper.

How sad it is to see the sacrament of salvation, the Church, operated like an earthly kingdom! From the power-plays of cardinals and bishops to gain more authority within the curia to the pastor of a small parish who makes every decision and dismisses any dissenting ideas or spiritualities, the Church has attracted many power-hungry men and women over its two millennia. A look to the history of the popes would scandalize even the most worldly of people! *What do they know of Christ?* One of my favorite moments of seminary came during one of my history classes studying the debauchery around one of the councils. The professor taught us how this faction didn't like that faction, and so a deacon from one attacked another in an alley behind the church building, attempting to effectively steal the council. Really horrible stuff. A student raised his hand, joking yet clearly distraught, and asked, "Professor, were any of these men Christian?" The laughter that ensued quickly faded to silence as the disappointment in our Church leaders sunk in. *Really. What do they know of Christ?*

We've all heard the saying, "Power corrupts and absolute power corrupts absolutely." This is the case for business leaders, politicians, and families, but it is also the case for the Church. It doesn't matter the setting, when people find themselves as rulers over a kingdom—a position in which they have or seek complete authority over others—they betray the Gospel that Jesus taught and turn into what he preached against. Power is a god. It is a false sense of security that gives people the impression that they are in control, that they do not need anyone else. It does not seek to be shared, but preserved, and when someone's authority is called into question, especially when the person wielding it does not want to relinquish it, violence is sure to follow. Power, sought for its own sake, is antithetical to follow Christ.

As Christians, we have but one kingdom and one king. While we may be entrusted with certain tasks of stewarding God's creation and should take our responsibilities seriously, we must also remember that no kingdom of earth can stand against heaven and that every authority on earth finds its source in God. To the extent that we forget this, clinging to our own kingdoms and our own power, we stand against God and become the tragic figure in Milton's *Paradise Lost* who finds it "better to reign in Hell than serve in Heaven." Power is such a false god that some would rather have it in a state of eternal isolation than give it up in a place of eternal bliss. This can be the case in our families, in our workplaces, in our Church, anywhere. Forcing others to submit to our rule, leading with authority rather than by service, turns us away from God because it turns us *into* a god.

There is only room enough in heaven for one God.

When we forget where we come from and where we go, it is only a matter of time before we forget that our role in the kingdom is not to rule over people but to serve with humility, just as Jesus did. He did not come with power and might. He did not submit peoples under his rule. He didn't command armies to protect him. No, he came in humility and meekness, serving the poorest of the world, and willingly gave up his life. In other words, he ruled by renouncing his power.

If we want to be his disciples, we must do the same. Let go of our powers and authorities, give up our desire to be in control, and seek to serve in all that we do.

The Powerlessness of the Cross

In our world, "might makes right." We value those with power and believe it is a commodity that one must possess in order to accomplish anything. Given the chaos of free will, we must have the ability to define, control, and enforce the way things should be. It is a necessary evil, we tell ourselves, that someone must wield power over others, and if we are responsible, it can actually be a good thing to possess it ourselves. *Think about all that we could do if we had more money or influence. If only we could get a Christian elected president. If only we could control Congress or the Supreme Court, we could use our power for the good of Christ.* The lure of power has tempted Christians for centuries, convincing us that it is something to be sought, something to be defended, something to be used to spread the reign of God.

This is a complete contradiction to our faith.

Seeing the evil of the world and how it failed to bring truth or life, Jesus preached of a radically different kingdom, instituting a new reign on earth. In many ways, what he did was found a revolution. But unlike the revolutions of our day, Jesus's movement did not involve a violent coup, insurgent uprising, or civil war; he did not ride into Jerusalem on an impressive horse with sword in hand; he was not accompanied by legions of armies, boasting of his power. Quite the opposite, actually. He used no violence and expressly forbade even hating one's enemy; his entry into Jerusalem was on a meek donkey, hardly the symbol of power and authority; his followers were the weak and poor, the ordinary and ritually unclean. Normally when we think of successful revolutions, we imagine leaders who are powerful and efficient, taking what they want with force, replacing the unjust rulers with their own. Jesus's revolution did include the shedding of blood, but only his own: Without a fight and with no defense, he willingly submitted to his enemies and was sacrificed as a criminal.

What defined Jesus's mission was not the proper use of power, but the very act of *powerlessness*. In his Beatitudes, he didn't just say that the poor and meek were to be included among the rest, that they were to be accepted among the rich and powerful. No, he said that "theirs is the kingdom of heaven" and "they will inherit the earth."

The poor and the meek, the peacemakers, and those who are perse-cuted—essentially, those who are without power—are the rightful recipients of the kingdom.

Jesus, himself, is the perfect embodiment of these Beatitudes, humbling himself from his heavenly throne to become like us in all things but sin. He chose to be born to an insignificant woman in an insignificant part of the world, wielding no power or influence but remaining as an outcast in society. When persecuted and wrongly condemned, he did not return insult for insult; in fact, when his own follower tried to defend him, cutting off the ear of the temple aide, Jesus admonished him and healed the aide's ear. In the end, he willingly laid down his life, offering the ultimate act of powerlessness for his disciples to follow. At no point in his ministry, even when it might have seemed fit to call on hordes of angels and attack the evildoers, he never once made a show of power. Instead, everything he said and did pointed to the same mission: emptying himself and remaining weak.

For most of us, this is beyond comprehension. We are told from a young age that we must be strong and that it is unbecoming to show emotions in front of others. Clichés flood our minds, telling us that "pain is weakness leaving the body" and that "God helps those who help themselves." Survival is for the "fittest," and so our goal is to be as self-sufficient as we can be, seeking help from no one and being our own masters. To show weakness is to fall behind. Power, more than anything else, is what we need to be free and happy.

This desire for power, even to be used for good things, is a complete contradiction to the cross. At the core of everything we believe is the idea that death brings new life. I'm not sure where the idea of "God helps those who help themselves" came from, but it could not be further from the cross and could not be any less biblical! All throughout Scripture, we hear of a God who actually *ignores* those who can help themselves and instead goes to the lost, forgotten, lowly, and weak, precisely because they cannot help themselves! Jesus brought us salvation, not through an amazing act of power and might, not by being in control and forcing evildoers to submit to the power of God. No, he accomplished this by being entirely vulnerable and weak. He did absolutely *nothing* to defend himself. The cross—the symbol of our faith and the goal for each and every Christian—is a reminder that salvation comes through powerlessness.

As tempting as it may be to want to be in control, as much as the world tells us we need to be powerful in order to be successful, our faith tells us otherwise. It is only when we are weak, when we ask for help, when we are meek and humble in the face of oppression, that we will be successful. How can this possibly be? Because only in those times, when we fully relinquish our own power, do we allow Christ to be strong in us. Just as the Father raised Jesus from the tomb in his moment of vulnerability, so, too, does God raise us up when we imitate Christ. On the road of discipleship, salvation is not won through our own ability, but given as a gift to those who are vulnerable enough to ask for it.

Kneeling before Jesus and asking, "What must I do to inherit eternal life," each and every one of us would likely hear this one thing. In one way or another—the way we lean upon our statuses, assert our independence, or seek to rule our own kingdoms—we all cling to some form of power in our lives. Let them go. Let go of anything and everything that lets us believe we are in control, that we determine our own faith, that we deserve love and respect from others, that we are all that we need. It is a ridiculous notion for anyone to believe that he or she is an island; for a Christian, it is a complete contradiction to everything we believe.

Let go of your power, let Christ be all the strength you need, and follow after him.

What Must I Do?

1. In what way do your many statuses—professional, familial, ecclesial, economic—offer you a sense of power over others? How does it affect the way you see yourself? How does it affect the way that you treat others?

2. Have you ever felt so helpless in your life that you had to rely on others to get by? What was the experience like? What can it teach you about Christian discipleship?

3. Reflect on the meaning of the cross, particularly as an act of powerlessness. How does Jesus' act of sacrifice fit into the way the world works? How might you emulate this self-sacrifice in your own life?

Let Go. Now.

If your hand causes you to sin, cut it off. It is better for you to enter into life maimed than with two hands to go into Gehenna, into the unquenchable fire. And if your foot causes you to sin, cut it off. It is better for you to enter into life crippled than with two feet to be thrown into Gehenna. And if your eye causes you to sin, pluck it out. Better for you to enter into the kingdom of God with one eye than with two eyes to be thrown into Gehenna, where "their worm does not die, and the fire is not quenched."

—MARK 9:43-48

I had a spiritual director once who told me to pray as if my life depended on it. Make prayer so unequivocally the most important thing in my life, he said, that you treat it as if you might cease to exist without it. While seemingly hyperbolic at first, dramatically phrased to emphasize the necessity of prayer, his words were not to be taken in any other way than literally. "Because, really, doesn't your life depend on it?" Everything we have, everything we are, everything we hope to become is the result of God's grace. We have no existence apart from God, for God is our life and our salvation, the one who holds our very being together. Prayer is not simply something that we do, it is a relationship and acknowledgement of Being itself.

Few people approach their lives with such urgency. For the most part, things go well for us, and there is little cause for alarm. We are able to rely on our own strength and ability to be fairly successful, suffer no extraordinary loss on a regular basis, and find our lives almost never in question. As it is, life is stable. With a general sense of satisfaction, we see no reason for major changes, no reason to shake things up, no reason to panic. Sure, we have flaws and are prone to sin—nobody's perfect!—but because things are going well, we can't help but see ourselves as generally good people trying our best. We pray and go to Church; we believe in Jesus and say that we want to do his will, and that seems like enough.

Is it though?

In my experience, we are comfortable being "mostly" Christian. We love the majority of what Jesus says and generally want to be a part of his Church but are also comfortable keeping one foot slightly out the door. We are in…but not *completely* in. There's that one thing, those few small flaws that we just can't get over, and so we just accept it. Looking at the overall commitment to the mission, we are okay hiding something from Jesus, reserving a bit of ourselves from our efforts. *It's just a small thing! I'm on board with everything else!* And so we see no reason to put much effort into it.

In one of his many extraordinary works of contemplation, Thomas Merton rails against the complacency of faith with a rather piercing image: being killed by one person makes you just as dead as being killed by an entire army. His point is that it is not enough to be a "good person" who "mostly" does the right thing; it takes but one mortal sin, one fatal flaw, one stumbling block of faith to forfeit eternal life. The rich young man of the Gospels was undoubtedly a "good person" who prayed to God and followed the law. By all accounts, he had but the one flaw, his attachment to his possessions. He was doing fine in life and could easily have justified this one flaw by looking at all of the good things he did otherwise. And yet, it only took one stumbling block to send him away. The rich young man was so attached to his possessions that even just this *one* flaw was enough to get in his way of following Jesus.

I wonder, sometimes, if we really grasp what's at stake here. *Our eternal lives are on the line.* As difficult as it is to sacrifice things in our lives that bring us happiness or comfort, what good is being happy or comfortable now if it is at the expense of our lives in heaven? Jesus tells us that if our eye causes us to sin that we should pluck it out, and I don't think he was joking. This is not hyperbole. If something in our lives prevents us from following Jesus with our whole hearts and taking up the mission of the kingdom, there is truly nothing more important in the entire world than removing it from our lives. Clinging to something that does not bring us life means clinging to our sure death.

Let go. Right now.

Throughout this book, I have offered seven stumbling blocks that get in the way of Christian discipleship and twenty-one examples of things that we cling to at the expense of our own lives. I have tried to be thorough in my reflection, but I recognize that these things do not wholly encompass all that we will face as disciples, nor are they all experienced in quite the same way by us all. As I said in the introduction, my hope in writing as I have is not to offer a mere checklist to be followed, a set of laws to fulfill to offer a false sense of assurance; this book is not meant to encapsulate an entire examination of conscience, covering all that might keep us from Jesus. No, my hope with this reflection is simply to prime the pump. I want to shock the system and energize you to dive headlong into being disciples. This book is not the end, but the start of taking each and every moment of your life seriously, of recognizing that a life in Christ is not simply about avoiding sin but being completely free to follow him whenever he calls and wherever he goes. Being a Christian is not lived simply at Church and in prayer, but in every facet of our lives. From the way we talk to our subordinates at work to the clothes we buy at the store, from the choices we make in buying a house to the way we spend our free time, all of it is an opportunity to let go of our own missions in life to follow Christ in his.

I asked the question in the introduction, and I have asked it throughout, but I will conclude by asking it once more: If you were to kneel at the feet of Jesus seeking eternal life, what would he tell you to let go of? Take this question to prayer. Reflect on the examples I have given. Listen for the voice of Christ in all that you do and take seriously what you hear. The stakes are too high to be just a "good person," someone who is "mostly" on board with Jesus. Find what gets in the way of following Jesus with your whole heart, and let go. Now.

ABOUT THE AUTHOR

Casey Cole, OFM, is a vowed religious in the Order of Friars Minor, commonly known as the Franciscans. He has a degree in religious studies with a minor in poverty studies from Furman University. In August 2017, he professed his final vows within the Order of Friars Minor; in June 2019 he was ordained a priest. Casey works extensively on social media, evangelizing and catechizing through YouTube videos, podcasts, and blog posts. (breakinginthehabit.org) and is currently the campus minister of the Catholic Center at the University of Georgia. He is the author of *Called: What Happens after Saying Yes to God*.